£10

# Nothing Being Everything

Also by Tony Parsons

*The Open Secret*
*As It Is*
*All There Is*

# Nothing Being Everything

Dialogues from Meetings
in Europe 2006/2007

Tony Parsons

First published in Great Britain 2007
by Open Secret Publishing

For contact details, please visit: www.theopensecret.com

Cover illustration adapted from a series of paintings
*Inner Landscapes* by John Miller

Interior layout and cover design: Julian Noyce

Printed by Antony Rowe Ltd, Chippenham, Wiltshire

A catalogue record for this book is available
from the British Library

ISBN-10: 0-9533032-2-3
ISBN-13: 978-0-9533032-3-6

All there is is this ...

being

the one appearing as two
nothing appearing as everything
the absolute appearing as the particular
emptiness appearing as fullness
the uncaused appearing as the caused
unicity appearing as separation
subject appearing as object
the singular appearing as plurality
the impersonal appearing as personal
the unknown appearing as the known

It is silence sounding and stillness moving
and these words appearing as pointers to the
wordless

... and yet nothing is happening

# Foreword

We appear to live in a world inhabited by individuals who, to a greater or lesser extent, have free will, choice and the ability to take action which brings about consequences. This reality is almost universally accepted without question.

For certain you are someone reading these words and it will definitely be your choice to stop or continue reading ... or so it seems.

In simple terms, it appears that our choice will be directed towards the attainment of pleasure and the avoidance of pain. We learn that, with the application of intelligent effort, we stand a better chance of making our lives work. This is the principle that apparently motivates most personal and global activity.

As the world we live in can seem threatening, we gather in various groups and create sets of rules which bring some sort of order and protection. Conflict and tension arise and our negotiations are not always successful.

Some of us seek a deeper meaning and purpose to life which can bring us hope and comfort. Out of this need, religious aspiration is born together with the belief in deity and a search for spiritual enlightenment.

Although these kinds of remedies can be effective for a while, they seem limiting in nature and do not, for some people, provide a profound and lasting fulfilment. The possible reason for this lack is given in *Nothing Being Everything*, together with an explanation of how the brain presumes, in early infancy, that there is a "world out there" which is separate to its host organism. In order to protect itself it apparently simulates a centre or a "self", from which negotiations and control can seem to be administered. Of course this construct of apparent individuality includes absolute belief and investment in free will, choice and the ability to act.

So, it appears that our whole way of living is grounded on a fundamental belief system which could be seen to be generated out of an assumption about reality, which is questionable.

Is it possible, for instance, that this reality is simply and only a unified and totally impersonal dynamic devoid of all intention, direction or purpose, but which paradoxically is the source and expression of vibrant passionate aliveness. Also, that within that expression, the apparent story of individuality manifests only as a meaningless reflection of its source.

This possibility would completely overturn the firmly established beliefs and values upon which we base our behaviour, and it would also undermine the very idea that we even have any choice about that behaviour.

It could be argued that the formulation of individuality is a very natural and inevitable process, so there is no need to enquire any further into its origin. And so, you could discard this book out of hand here and now ... but what would be discarding it? Would it be you, or would it be its source?

Is our cause and purpose simply a dream? If so it seems that the awakening from that dream could be a disaster. There would be no-one left to run their lives and possibly no managing director of the universe to offer guidance. So, if our life is lost then everything is lost, and there is only emptiness. But could it be that, like a vacuum, emptiness is suddenly absolute fullness ... simply nothing being everything?

# Preface

It's a safe bet, I suspect, that many readers who find themselves drawn to this new treasure of unfiltered aliveness – *Nothing Being Everything* – will have logged more than a few miles on the long and winding road of devotedly seeking for that which could never be lost ... a self-reinforcing paradox that fuels the world of seeking.

As such, the vibrantly alive expressions of freedom that follow will typically be read from one of two broad perspectives. Either these words will be filtered through the lens of separation, anticipating that one essential insight might bring oneness and absolution for the seeker, or this radical communication may instead be received ... and celebrated ... as the ever-present and boundless immediacy of life simply happening on its own, with no agent or destination anywhere to be found.

Indeed, the profound simplicity of the open secret, so beautifully and powerfully pointed to in these pages, is always one step too near for the mind and "understanding" to ever approach. Herein lies the invitation to give the deductive analytical mind a rest and simply breathe in these words with the natural, effortless rhythm and resonance from which they arose. The unmistakable scent of remembrance of that most intimate of all things, so energetically and uncompromisingly present in these dialogues, is intuited most directly in the absence of the idea of there being anything to figure out or get.

Over the past decade or so, a wave of interest and appreciation for teachings of a "non-dual" persuasion has swept through the upper rafters of the spiritual pantheon. This interest has exposed the purely dualistic visions of earning worthiness for release from the wheel of suffering that form the plea and implied promise of almost all of spirituality and religion. And yet, save for a rare handful of exceptions, almost all the popular "non-dual-like" facsimiles on the current satsang circuit cater to the demands and expectations of the separate individual conditioned by the seduction of process and progression. Not so the open secret.

Such teachings of accommodation are often offered under the rationale, benevolently arrogant as it may be, of "stepping down to meet all the unawakened people halfway up the mountain", and thereby continually reinforce fundamentally dualistic misconceptions as hierarchy and a personal evolution.

This conundrum, in turn, presents a fundamental and subliminal reaffirmation for the seeker that they are indeed lost and in need of salvation. As Tony Parsons conveys again and again throughout his books, this is an absolutely unworkable bargain for the mind that can never find the home it so desperately looks for. For some, when this news is first really heard, it can bring a transient wave of despair, as all the hoped for and projected ideals of "becoming divine and exalted" crash and burn in the boundless ocean of there only being just this – life happening – with no personal markers on which to hang such attributes of attainment.

However, even in that first surprise of spontaneous recognition, what at times is initially overlooked is the unspeakable impersonal freedom that stands revealed in the timeless light of no-thing being everything. Not a detached pseudo-freedom conjured from a "spiritually sanctioned" avoidance of life, but from the innate immediacy of remembrance that there has truly never been a separate entity to whom this is all happening ... what a joyful revolution!

This is about paradox in the extreme, and that paradox simply loses its apparent power to obscure in the light of rediscovery of this primal innocence that is the open secret. A true paradox in that it is constantly being lived in full by, and as, everyone, and yet remains thoroughly hidden as the essential secret of life as long as there is a "someone" looking for it.

It's little wonder then that the vast majority of the world's wisdom teachings, including many recent therapeutic offshoots, all aim to resolve this mystery in a kind of progressive, linear fashion for the individual who is either overtly (or covertly as with many popular pseudo-non-dual teachings) taken for granted as the central locus of the universe ... i.e. the presumed one that needs to gain insight and understanding for that individual to become free.

Indeed, those teachings that do pay lip service to non-dual concepts often present a more subtle, even subliminal, confirmation of this core misperception, and thus inadvertently reinforce the illusory sense of separation all the more.

It is this ever-present reality of there only being life ... as it is ... that Tony Parsons so directly and powerfully exposes. This is Tony's rare and unique gift ... the clear expression of a revolutionary vision fuelled by an energetic aliveness of freedom that simply can't and won't compromise. Tony is an expert marksman ... a skeet shooter of unparalleled acumen ... destroying one "yes but" clay pigeon in flight after another, leaving nowhere for the mind to go ... leaving nowhere to seek refuge from the boundlessness of simply Being.

For many long-time veterans of gurus and sangas of one kind or another, a weekend or residential with Tony is like a breath of fresh air, as one time-honoured thread of confusion after another unravels and evaporates in the open, effortless humour of dear friends meeting together. All offered with no agenda, expectation or demands of any kind, just the heartfelt joy of sharing this most amazing of all gifts ... that you never "owned a life" to begin with that required defending and working out.

When a readiness to hear such a direct and un-adorned message meets such uncompromising clarity, something else might step out of the shadows of becoming into the quiet and gentle light of timeless aliveness that is this open secret.

The essential message of the open secret has been laid out fully in Tony's prior three books, and yet this latest collection – *Nothing Being Everything* – reflects the ever-fresh interplay and symbiosis between yet more subtle and mature questions and in response the natural honing down of clarity of expression.

As such, those most intimately familiar with Tony's arresting way with words will find much to savour and treasure here, and *Nothing Being Everything* is sure to take its place alongside his other works as a singular and revolutionary communication.

*Shannon Dickson*
*March 2007*

# 1

Until your life is lost you will always wonder why... for that which is sought has never been lost and what the seeker tries to understand can never be known.

That is why there is nothing in the open secret message for the seeker to grasp and claim ownership of ... no special states of bliss, stillness or presence are on offer.

The fallacy of the need to attain earnestness, acceptance or refinement of the body-mind is exposed. You will not be invited to look within and discover "your true nature" or that state of awareness which promises so much but comes and goes so quickly. There are no spiritual lollipops of any kind on offer here.

There is no compromise with the seeker's need for guidance, process or teachings of becoming. There are no special mummies and daddies here, no spiritual families to belong to. There is no magic, no charisma, no transference of any kind ... nothing is for sale but the fairy story of the little "me" could expire.

The gift of being together in this palpable boundlessness is that already what you are is seen as wholeness, without expectations or demands. Confusion and resistance can dissolve in the light of openness and nothing will be left. Out of that nothingness emerges the indescribable fullness and wonder of simply being.

○  ○  ○

*So where does this information come from? Is it that our conversation is a conversation with myself? And myself tells me that all this is a dream?*

It's nothing speaking to nothing. The nothing over there is pretending it's somebody. It's as simple as that. But the words – these words – won't necessarily create an awakening there; these are just concepts. We're sharing words together. There's something much more powerful going on in this room. There's a sense of boundlessness that arises in these meetings. But somewhere the words may go to the dreamer and the dreamer will convert them into what they want to hear. They won't listen to what's being said because they don't want to hear that there is no-one. It is too threatening.

So continually we find that people come to these meetings and absolutely don't hear what's being said. The fundamental thing that is being said here is hardly ever heard. This is the hidden message that's only available when there's a readiness. But it's hidden under everything else. You have Christianity, Buddhism, traditional Advaita, so-called non-dualism being taught everywhere. There are many books and teachings which claim to be Advaita teachings but which continuously compromise the fundamental and frightening mystery held within the essence of the word Advaita. This message is about the death of the separate individual, and its avoidance or compromise comes straight out of self-survival.

*Does it make any sense then to make any effort in life?*

As a dreamer it seems convincing that you are an individual who can make an effort to get from A to B. In reality there is no you and no A or B. But going even deeper than that, there is no-one that can make an effort and there is no-one that can give up seeming to make an effort. The difficulty with this message is that people suggest that Tony Parsons is saying that you don't have to do anything. The message is not that there is someone who can't do anything or doesn't need to. This message is not that at all. This message is that there is no separate one with free will and choice. There's a fundamental difference.

*Did you always know this?*

Oh no, I never knew it. I still don't. But there was a sense of this. This is the communication of unknowing. Here is nothing talking about nothing. There is no-one to know this and nothing to know.

*But it seems I have a choice because I can work or I can sleep. I can do what I want. So it seems to me I have a choice. If I want to go, I could go, or stand up. I have some choice.*

So that's the dream. There is the dreamer dreaming that they are definitely choosing to stand up or not. The idea of standing up will arrive and the dreamer will stand up and thinks it's choosing to stand up. It's the dream. You've never done anything. There's no-one that's ever done anything. All there is, is what is happening ... to no-one.

*It could happen in a better way!*

*(laughs)* Yes. It can be an uncomfortable struggle. It's uncomfortable all the time there's someone there trying to find something. When it's discovered there's no-one, there's just a celebration of aliveness by no-one. There's just aliveness. And it can't be avoided. You can't escape aliveness. No-one can escape this because everybody already is it. So it wouldn't matter if you stood up and walked out of this room right now. Standing up and walking out of this room is what's happening. It's aliveness. There is only that. There is only being.

*And what about responsibility then?*

There is no responsibility. There is no-one. No-one is responsible. No-one's ever done anything so no-one is responsible. Everything that's apparently happened has apparently happened.

*But responsibility happens.*

Dreaming happens and the idea that there is a separate someone happens. It's a dream. And the idea that they are responsible and there's such a thing as cause and effect also arises in that dream.

o  o  o

*What is death?*

At death all that ends is the idea of time and story and the struggle to find liberation, simply because in separation the whole mechanism of the body-mind organism is searching for oneness. When that apparent organism ceases to function, which it does at death, then the whole story of searching to find oneness is no more and there is oneness.

o  o  o

*I heard your wife say that you were very passionate about this, Tony.*

Look at the whole world we're apparently living in. It's about passion. It's total aliveness. And it's all about the childlike wonder of this. That's all it's about. It has no other meaning. It's not a battle between good and evil. It's not a story about going anywhere. It's just a passionate explosion of aliveness. That's all it is. It's just a passionate explosion of beingness which is telling those who think they are separate people that there is only freedom.

All the time, right at this moment, everybody in this room is being bombarded by love through the senses, through everything that is. And the beloved is saying, "Look, you don't have to become anything or change or do anything ... I am here already." It's so stunning you see. It's so stunningly simple and direct. It's just this. But we're always looking for something else out there. Some concept, some idea that we should be better. "I've got to be better." And the lover, the perfect lover, is sitting on our shoulder filling us with aliveness, saying, "No you don't have to be anything, what you are is already wholeness."

There is only immaculate wholeness and that is all there is. It's amazing.

o   o   o

*You're saying that boredom and depression are aliveness?*

Being bored ... this is oneness being bored and depressed. It can't be anything else. Liberation is totally all-inclusive.

*It's looked upon in a certain way by the mind, isn't it?*

Oh yes. The whole idea, for instance, of being enlightened is looked upon in a certain way by the mind. You know, it's all about being very beautiful and loving and forgiving and accepting and still and quiet. Bullshit! That's such a prison.

*With the mind, I say, there is just this, and then the mind's just fallen away and there's just this. So the mind kinda bows down.*

Yes it does. It gets on its knees and gives up.

*Falls away.*

And takes its place in the manifestation.

*Yes. So it's just the recognition.*

It is being this, within which recognition happens.

But what I'm trying to say is there isn't any one that can bring that about.

*Yes, it's like itself recognising itself.*

Yes, that happens, but being is still beyond that recognition whilst including it.

*Sometimes I have heard that the mind can actually bring you to this place.*

No, absolutely not. The mind is only a storyteller and can't possibly comprehend timelessness.

*But it can lead you a little bit.*

No it can't. Thinking can't comprehend being, it only arises in being. I'm using words and understanding can bring clarity. But clarity isn't awakening. Clarity isn't liberation. Clarity is just another possession.

*But, and at the same time, it is the recognition.*

Again, liberation, being, is beyond recognition. The conceptual recognition that there is no-one is nothing … it's a transient idea.

○ ○ ○

*Tony, I don't understand the difference between awakening and liberation.*

There is no such thing as awakening or liberation but these terms are used to describe something that only *appears* to happen to no-one. Awakening is what invariably seems to happen to most apparent seekers, but you can't say it's in every case, because there are

7

no certainties about anything. But what seems to happen is that there's a sudden timeless seeing by no-one that there is only oneness, and for a while it seems that there is still a subtle seeker who doesn't understand what's just happened but wants to own it. And then apparently it's possible that it's suddenly realised by no-one that the seeker who wants to claim oneness is also oneness, and then it's all over, then there's no-one. There's nothing but being.

It's like when you were tiny, tiny children there is only being. And then a moment of separation comes and you're weaned out of being, because young children still sense what being is like, even after that moment of separation, when the ego or the sense of self develops and grows, and we come into the world of the individual. There is a period where there's still a sense of beingness.

And then it seems to be lost. But for some people, when awakening happens, there's a weaning back into being. It's so difficult when you answer questions because it sounds like something that's happening in time and it's real. In fact none of it is real. There is no such thing as liberation or awakening. All there is is being.

*There must be a strategy. There must be a formula. If only I had the formula. Wouldn't it be correct to say if I found out how the mind's working ...*

Absolutely not. What we're talking about here has no relationship to the mind. The mind is just a voice on the side that has all sorts of ideas, but can't possibly conceive beingness because the mind is a moving part. It functions only in story, within being.

*So there's nothing to do really ... well, of course not.*

But in a sense what happens is that there's a knowing of that ... as we were saying, primarily there is a knowing of this. So you can sit on that chair and know that your bum is on the seat, for instance. Or that there's a sound outside. There's a knowing, an awareness of what's happening in your body, there's a knowing that thinking is happening ... thinking "I'm trying to get this", may be happening. You can feel life in your body right now. There's an energy of aliveness in this room right now. Nobody could deny that exists. But there's a knowing of that energy.

*But still in the dream.*

Absolutely. There is still the knowing, the awareness that you're sitting there and that knowing awareness is still in the dream.

*So what will happen?*

What *can* happen is that there can be a knowing you're sitting there, and then there can be a shift where there is just sitting there. That's the shift. That's the timelessness. In a sense, everything that's happening in this room seems to be happening to you in time. Actually it is timeless being, it is the gift. So all the time you're being bombarded through your senses with timeless being. You breathe, you see, you hear, you feel, you taste that which you constantly seek elsewhere. Whatever's happening is oneness, or beingness saying, "Look, there's only this. You don't have to look. It's already all there is!"

*So what will happen when ...*

Well what happens is that already in that moment of there being no-one and there just being what's happening, light has entered the apparent darkness and the light dissipates the darkness. The darkness is dissipated and apparently falls away. The me, the separation, simply disintegrates in that light. And then there's nothing left.

o   o   o

*Where does the idea of being separated come from?*

Everything is nothing arising as everything, including the idea of separation.

*To make this separation go away there is an effort, yes? People are trying to ...*

Oh, yes. But the trying fuels the separation. The whole reinforcement of the individual is in that attempt to find oneness. That effort goes on reinforcing a sense of separation from oneness.

*And that is a joke isn't it?*

That is why all teachings based on the idea of spiritual endeavour or choice are actually teachings of imprisonment because they go on imprisoning the person in something called "being a separate person".

*So for the mind there is no way out?*

Well, this has got nothing to do with the mind. When apparent liberation happens then the mind takes its natural place in the functioning ... it's no longer the great power.

# 2

So, you can't get away from what you're looking for because there's no escape from everything. This is all there is so how can anyone lose this? How does anybody have to attain being when this is all and everything?

What's apparently happening? What's happening is you're sitting on a chair breathing, seeing this, hearing a voice, that's what's happening. That is this. This is all there is. And if you get up and walk out of this room that will be this. And if you don't really hear what's being said, that will be this. And if there's a real hearing of what's being said, that will be this. And tonight when you go home and eat your dinner, that will be this. There's no escape from this. There's no escape from being. There is only being.

This is being, being a room, being bodies on chairs, being Tony Parsons waving his arms around. That's all there is.

This is a very rare and revolutionary message. Some people say, "Oh well you're saying what a lot of other people are saying".

Absolutely not.

If this is really heard, if the fundamental secret is heard somewhere, *"you"* won't ever hear it, but if it's heard it will be seen that this is a rare and revolutionary message. It's about the rediscovery that there is no such thing as separation. There is no separate one. There is no other. There's nothing to be separate from. There's no-one who can be separate. This is all and everything. What is sought has never been lost.

However, in the everything arises the idea of separation – "Oh I am a person. I am definitely a separate person. I'm an individual and my mother and my father and priests and the teachers and the bosses and the wives and the husbands are all telling me that I am a separate person who can make a choice for better or worse." So there continues a searching for better or worse. The dreamer is created.

The dreamer is the apparent separate individual. "I am a person." That's the dreamer. And that dreamer can only function in that dream of being separate. And so it grows up with a world of dreamers who all say, "This is your life, this is your own life and you can make a choice to make it better or worse. You actually have free will to choose better or worse."

And somewhere for many, many people – more and more people these days – that is not the answer. Somewhere there's a knowing that there's a discomfort about that sense of being separate. There's something lost. Something isn't whole.

And you can go to religion, you can go to therapy, you can go all over the place, and try and fill that sense of loss. You can go to a teacher of enlightenment and try and fill that sense of loss. But all the time those people are saying to you, "Yes, you are a separate individual" ... you stay locked in the prison – in the dreamer's prison ... the dreamer's prison of being a separate person who needs to find something ... There's nothing to find. This is it. There is only this. And by "this" I mean what seems to be happening, beingness.

You come in here as an apparent separate individual, let's presume you do, and you're sitting there looking for something. It's already this. Whatever seems to be happening is this. There is only this. And whatever is happening is not happening to anyone in this room. There is no-one in this room to whom anything is happening. There is just happening. This is space. This is emptiness. This is nothing. What's sitting here is nothing and what's arising in that nothing is the sense of a body, hearing noises, feeling feelings, thinking. Thinking also happens to no-one. Nobody has ever thought anything because there is no-one. So thinking is happening, feeling is happening, listening to this voice is happening.

All there is, is life happening. All there is, is aliveness. Aliveness is beingness. There isn't anything other than that. It may be suddenly seen that all that's sitting there is aliveness. Nobody can teach you to be alive. Who would have the arrogance to teach you to *be* when there is only being? Who would have the arrogance to say you have to change? There is only nothing and everything. This is beyond understanding, beyond the heart and mind of man.

And we can talk together and use words but the words will only point – go on pointing – to something beyond. The words may destroy the illusion in the mind that there is separation because the mind is the storyteller. What can fall apart here is the idea that there is such a thing as a separate individual. And of course what also falls apart is the idea that there's anything that needs to be done, that there's anyone that ever did anything.

So, there is nothing to attain, nothing to understand and what is being is this. Simply this aliveness arising for no-one.

Liberation is an energetic shift. It's a shift from the contraction of being someone, a separate person with a world out there, back into the natural and very ordinary sense of there only being everything. So that contraction expands out into everything and this thing you thought you were becomes everything.

This communication has nothing to do with Tony Parsons. This is not something that Tony Parsons owns or has achieved. It's got nothing to do with knowing, personal endeavour or achievement. Tony Parsons is no different to anyone else in this room. It's just a body-mind organism that waves its arms around and talks.

The difficulty is that in seeking we personalise everything. We try to say, "What's in this for me? What can I get out of this? What do I have to do to be this?" That's the confusion. You don't have to do anything because you – this – is already being done. It's being done. Aliveness is happening. Being is simply being.

And once this seeker, that always thinks it has to find something and discover something new or different, falls away, suddenly there is a total relaxation and dropping into the sheer joy of being this. Not the knowing of being, but simply, directly being.

And people say to us when apparent awakening happens, "It's so funny. For years I've searched for bliss and peace and all those other things that are on offer. All those years I searched for that, and what I didn't realise was that what I was looking for already is this. It's always been here. It never left me. It's the perfect lover."

But let's talk together about it. And when you ask a question you won't get an answer. In a sense you'll get an answer but the answer will continually bring the questioner back to the realisation that there is just this. The whole answer to life is that there is no answer. There is only life.

This isn't my truth. It's not a truth. There is no truth. This is just an exposure, a description of that which is the only constant. It is a rediscovery. And the utter simplicity of it confounds the mind. We will hear this afternoon the mind battling with this ... because the mind loves a story. The mind wants to be in a story about seeking and finding. And what's being shared today is that there is nothing to find. This is already it.

○ ○ ○

*I wanted to ask you about awakening because we do experience it.*

Well nobody experiences awakening because nobody awakens. Awakening brings with it the realisation that there is nobody.

*And then it goes away again?*

Well no, it doesn't go away, you come back. There is only this and then there's something that comes back and says, "Well is this it?" All the traditional teachings are a denial that this is it because what they're really saying to you is, "In order to find enlightenment you have to become something". The very idea that you have to become something is a direct denial that already *this is all there is.*

So when awakening apparently happens to no-one, then the seeker comes back for a while, the subtle seeker comes back and says, "Well what was that? I don't know what it was but I want it". So you come back and it seems that what happened is no longer there. But in fact it is all and everything. And in a sense, later on, it is seen that the one that comes back, that wants to own that, is also that, and then it's all over.

*Why do we deny it or why do we go back?*

It is denied because there is a fascination in looking for it. It's a fascination. Oneness plays a joke on itself called "becoming a separate individual looking for something called 'not being a separate individual'". But it's totally fascinated by the whole search. It is the play of being. And once it is seen that there is all and everything there's no longer a question of why. All the time there is a seeker, the seeker is really basically saying, "Why have I lost paradise? Where is paradise?" But this is paradise. Even the looking for it, even the confusion, the seeking is totally immaculately the expression of the infinite. There's nowhere to go. There's nothing right or wrong. There's no above or below. There's no before and after. All there is is this. It's stunning.

○ ○ ○

*So this is always immediate and now.*

Well it's not now. There isn't a now. It is simply this. The timeless expression of the infinite.

*And whatever it is has no reality?*

It is both real and unreal. It's both the nothing and the something. The difficulty is that when we apparently become individuals, we seem to become something. "I am something. And everything else around me is something." And then there's a longing for something called "enlightenment". So "I am something that's going to find something called 'enlightenment'". But in reality there is both something and nothing. All that manifests is something and nothing together. And the separate something is incapable of seeing nothing. It's frightened of seeing nothing because nothing points to personal death. This is about dying. You haven't come here to get anything; you've come here to lose something ... the dream of you.

○ ○ ○

*If liberation happens is that guaranteed?*

Liberation is not something that happens ... it already is. But for the seeker it is believed it isn't. When there is no seeker it is seen by no-one that there is only liberation, there is only being. So at the depth of this, when the body-mind ceases to function as the dreamer, all there is is being.

*I was just wondering if you thought that, for instance, meditation was useful?*

Well who's going to meditate? And who would it be useful to?

*Sorry?*

Who is going to choose to meditate?

*Exactly. So it's irrelevant.*

Well, meditation is simply what it is and this message isn't about being against or for anything. So this message is not saying you shouldn't meditate or you should. It's saying that if meditation happens it happens but there is no-one that can make meditation happen. There's no-one in this room that can make themselves breathe or sit on the chair. There's no free will or choice at any level, except in the dream of separation.

*So it doesn't matter if I meditate or not.*

You are not really hearing what is being said here. Who is going to meditate and how is meditation going to matter?

○ ○ ○

*On one of your CDs, Tony, you mentioned that we were like divine puppets.*

Yes.

*Could you say a little bit more about that?*

The body-mind is simply an object. There's no-one in there. It's just a mechanism that works. It's an organism that grows up and works and is conditioned and has feelings, thoughts, preferences and habits that go on, and there's no-one in there doing that. That is simply oneness arising as a body-mind organism which is, in a way, a divine puppet in that it just responds and reacts to whatever's going on without any self-volition. However, there is no puppeteer. There is no script, no plan, no destiny, no fate ... it is all timeless being appearing as something seeming to happen.

○  ○  ○

*Tony, could you just speak about the phenomena of when people are getting messages from angels?*

It's only another appearance. It's just a story.

*A story?*

It's just an appearance. This room is an appearance. Listening to the news tonight is the same as talking to an angel. It has no relevance. The mind thinks that the angel is somehow from a special, heavenly place – but there is no special, heavenly place. There's nowhere else. So the angel is oneness angel-ing. But let's be clear about this, because oneness is very clever at creating

21

all sorts of reasons to keep the dream going, so it would appear in all sorts of forms like angels and ascended masters. Have you heard of ascended masters?

*Yes.* (laughing) *I'm just wondering because there are so many books around ...*

Yes, I've noticed. *(laughing)* There is an abundance of books about ascended masters available and it's all just another story which has no relevance to liberation. It is the guru-mind which sees these ideas as spiritually significant.

*So this is just happening in the mind of these people?*

Yes, it's all in the story. But then you see the whole appearance, in a way, is simply oneness appearing as whatever it is. It has absolutely no relevance to anybody. It's just this. It's no more relevant than that wall. The wall is being this and so is the angel. And also you have people apparently talking to the dead. It's the same sort of thing. It is all the play of being.

*Like channelling?*

Yes, so-called channelling. It's an appearance.

*Then channelling is possible?*

Well it seems anything is possible. The mind is capable of anything, except liberation from itself.

So oneness, through the mind, creates things like channelling and angels, ascended masters, all of this. It's just oneness. But, you know, the seeker is attracted to strange phenomena because it appears as some sort of magic. I know people who have gone to teachers and reported that the teacher has been on the stage and the teacher has vanished. And then the teacher might reappear and they vanish. *(laughing)* And then they become the teacher and see what the teacher sees. All of that goes on. It's all totally meaningless magic. But it's oneness appearing in all sorts of forms. Of course, one is seduced into the idea that this has something to do with enlightenment.

So you can go to teachers who have that sort of magic way of doing things. You can go to teachers who have great charisma. You can go to teachers who teach you all sorts of things to do. All you get here is nothing.

*Then let's take the mind away. Put the mind aside.*

Well who is going to put the mind aside? The dreamer can't put the mind aside because the dreamer is dreaming. The mind is the story maker ... "I am a dreamer looking for oneness." There is no such thing as a mind. All there is, is thinking. You think there's a thought, then a thought, then a thought. There is no such thing as the mind. But one of the thoughts is, "I am a separate person." And another thought is, "I can go somewhere called 'better than this'." That's how story-making happens.

The whole point of liberation is that it has nothing to do with the story. Liberation simply is, despite the story. Liberation is all there is, and in liberation arises the appearance of a story and the appearance, let's say, of a seeker looking for that which is beyond seeking. So, there's no connection. I know the mind would fondly like there to be a connection with what happened previously to what is being expressed. But what happened previously has no relevance to liberation. You can't creep up on oneness. You can't move nearer to everything. There is only everything. All the time you are trying to creep up to, or get nearer to being, or move along a path to being, you are being that is trying to move towards being.

*But the perception of that can't be gained by any kind of attempt to perceive what you're talking about. It just arises.*

Absolutely. It is heard or it isn't heard.

*There's nothing that an individual can do?*

No. That is not what is being said here! That idea implies that there *is an individual who cannot do anything*. The open secret is suggesting that there is no individual and therefore no volition of any kind ... except in the dream.

*But are you saying that there's just life and we all experience this?*

No, there's just life. Being is all there is.

*It's just life. We just think we're experiencing it.*

In life there are people who think it's their life and their experience. The separate individual believes, and experiences, that what is happening is happening to a central entity they call "me". But all there is is life happening ... apparently. It is totally and utterly simple.

*And totally and utterly meaningless.*

Utterly meaningless. Except to the apparent separate entity.

*But it doesn't actually matter.*

Nothing matters. Then you see, the apparent individual thinks "Oh well I can do anything". No you can't do anything because you can't do "being enlightened", you can't do "not being enlightened". You can't do anything because there is no individual volition. You can't do doing nothing. You can't do doing anything. There's no-one. In one way this message is incredibly liberating; in another way it's totally frustrating for the individual seeker. You can't go out of here now and raid a bank. Who's going to raid a bank?

○  ○  ○

*So Tony, nothingness, observing nothingness right, is this nothingness all-knowing?*

Not in the sense that we would think of as all-knowing, no. It doesn't need to be all-knowing because nothing is already everything. The sort of all-knowing that we think of as all-knowing is certainly not relevant because there is already nothing and everything. This is boundless being without cause so there's no need for information. This is the wonder of unknowing in which everything is already new. There's no need any more for information.

But you describe nothingness as a separate object out there somewhere whereas all and everything is nothingness. It is not something to be discovered, it already is being.

○  ○  ○

*They say there's no mind, just a bundle of thoughts in the ether or whatever ... I mean these thoughts that float around in this body-mind for example are very strange sometimes. Why are these thoughts floating around?*

Well what you're saying is why is there anything? Thoughts are no different to emotions, sounds or whatever. Thinking is just another part of what's happening. So thoughts arrive and to some extent have a power all the time there's someone taking delivery of them.

We grow up respecting what we call the mind, although there is no such thing. We respect most of the thoughts we have because we think they're going to get us to somewhere. All dream-thinking is about getting somewhere. "She loves me." "I'm going to be enlightened tomorrow." All of that is an anticipation. In one sense it's all about promoting the paradox of there being someone trying to get somewhere. But it is simply being arising as dream-thinking.

*But we're not generating this?*

No. Everything arises out of no-thing. It simply is what is apparently happening ... to no-one. Nobody has ever thought anything ... there is no-one.

○   ○   ○

*So is there just a surrendering and acceptance that in each moment everything that's happening and arising and occurring is exactly as it's meant to be?*

No, it's absolutely nothing to do with that. It's not

anything to do with acceptance. This has nothing to do with somebody accepting what is happening in the moment, because there is nothing happening, and there is no moment and there is no somebody.

*Is there any point in oneness acknowledging oneness?*

Oneness doesn't acknowledge oneness. There is only oneness. There is no action. All there is is this. Being is totally action-less and in it arises apparent action.

*If no-one knows what this particular wall looks like to Tony Parsons, there seems to be a sense of separateness.*

Yes.

*Which is contradictory or ... do you know what I'm trying to say?*

Yes. In the dream of being a separate individual everything arises uniquely because there is only that. So in that dream everything is totally uniquely for that apparent seeker. In liberation there is still that uniqueness. The difference is that there's no-one in there that that's happening to. It just is happening. And what is also seen is the mystery that it is no thing arising as uniqueness. It's totally incomprehensible. It can never be understood that in liberation, when there is no-one, when the whole separation has dropped away, there is still a celebration of the unique duality that appears to be arising. But that duality is seen as the play of being. So apparent duality is then celebrated.

*And so we're still celebrating?*

Apparent duality, or this world that we see, this

dream that we see, is then celebrated, by no-one.

*As duality and non-duality?*

There aren't two. Oneness arises as an appearance of two.

*It's a mystery, a paradox.*

Yes. You will never get this because *you're* there trying to get it. When there is no-one there is only being.

*Is it not mindlessness?*

No. Thinking still happens. There's nothing wrong with anything. In liberation everything can happen. There's nothing that's denied, including thinking. The whole idea that somehow thinking is divorced from oneness is just another ignorance. All there is is being thinking. "I want a cup of tea." "I'm going bankrupt." "She doesn't love me". Thoughts arise. A thought arises, another thought arises, another thought arises ... that is thinking happening and there are times when there is no thinking happening.

○   ○   ○

*So the aliveness that's me is the same as the aliveness that is her ...*

Absolutely. It's just aliveness. And it just arises seemingly in a richly different way, which is just stunning. But the different way that it arises is totally meaningless. It's just the absolute joy of oneness appearing as two and being apparently totally unique. Whatever happens right now, in the story, is unique. It will never happen again. It never has happened before. It's totally new. What's happening is totally new. It apparently comes and goes. It's alive and it's not. You're sitting in total newness. You're breathing total newness. You're thinking total newness. Nobody's ever spoken like this before. It's total uniqueness. Arising, falling away, arising, falling away. It's amazing.

*Tony, you've just said before and after, and that's time.*

There is no before and after.

*But you just said "It's never been thought before".*

Well, to try and describe this to someone who thinks there is a before, it's a stunning realisation that what is apparently arising is totally unique. It's another way of describing what people think of as something that happened before. What I'm trying to say is you, sitting on that seat, has never happened before. But I'm only speaking to someone who thinks there is a before. Just so, there is only this.

*I'm reminded of that quote from T S Eliot "At the still point of the turning world ... there the dance is". So it's really happening in stillness.*

And silence. This is stillness and silence. This is stillness moving and silence sounding. And it's totally new ... apparently.

○ ○ ○

*If someone were to ask me what I got out of this so far ...*

What, today you mean?

*Yes, now. Yes, today. Being here.*

Are you trying to get something out of it?

*Yes.*

Right. OK. Fine.

*Having never heard of you before, if someone asked me what you're saying ... what was the point of it, what was he talking about, I would say he was talking about the acceptance of the moment.*

*That's my perception of it. Is that wrong or right?*

It's not wrong or right; it's what's perceived there. But this is beyond acceptance and the moment, which are both stories. What is being suggested here is that there is no-one who can accept and there is no moment. Somehow a moment implies another moment. There is no moment. It's like the idea of being here now. There is no-one that can be here and there is no now. And there is no-one that can accept this. I'm not suggesting that you accept this because from this perception there is no separate you and there is nothing that needs doing. When the separate entity is no more it is seen that all there is is this.

*Did you, as Tony Parsons, arrive at this?*

I absolutely didn't arrive. That's the whole point of what we're talking about. What's being communicated here has nothing to do with Tony Parsons. Tony Parsons didn't arrive at this. That's the point. Tony Parsons is no more, in that sense, a seeker, a dreamer. So I haven't arrived anywhere. There's nowhere and no-one to arrive. But it is noticed that this is all there is.

*I'm a bit lost.*

That's fine. The whole point of being here is to get lost.

*I'm lost out there too.*

But it's possible that the one that's out there that feels lost will no longer be. This is not about learning to know something.

*If there is nothing, well there is nothing here either, right?*

Yes.

*It's all an illusion. It's a dream.*

I think when you say it's illusion I wouldn't use that term because I think that's a bit confusing. This is both real and unreal. The dreaming is the dream of separation.

*Right.*

If I told you that the wall was an illusion you might go and bang your head on it and it would still appear as a wall and so would your headache appear as a headache. But basically they are both nothing appearing as this.

*But it's just because I'm conditioned to know that this is a wall, that I would hurt my head.*

Not at all. There is no you. There is no conditioning. There is no wall. But in the appearance, there is you who can bang your head on a wall and it would hurt.

*Right. But it's like when I fall asleep in this life here, I have dreams and my dreams seem as if they're reality.*

Yes.

*There's things happening.*

Apparently.

*Next morning I wake up and I find, oh it was just a dream. Nothing happened.*

Yes. But when the seeker wakes up the next morning there is still another dream that now seems real. It is the dream of being a separate individual.

*Right. So this is the same kind of dream that I'm dreaming at night.*

The dream is whatever it is. It's an appearance.

*Yeah, it's a fantasy, is it?*

You could call it a fantasy if you want to. But it's the appearance. It's nothing appearing as your bedroom and your body, you in the bed or whatever.

*But in reality there is no body.*

There is a body appearing. But all the time there is someone, that separate individual is constantly looking for something, constantly longing for and fearing nothingness.

Because it lives in this dream of being something it thinks that what it longs for is lots of money or lovers, lots of somethings. But also in the end the final search is for something called "enlightenment". There isn't anything called "enlightenment" because there is only already that which is both nothing and everything.

The difficulty the dreamer has is it's always looking for what it longs for in something else and is never able to see nothing being everything, which is what it actually longs for and also fears. So it's totally in a fix ... a catch-22 situation.

*Yeah. Like a vicious circle almost?*

Yes it appears to be. All the time there is seeking it is secret ... it is also openly everything.

○ ○ ○

*So there is no Munich?* (laughing)

There is no Munich, no. There's no Munich, no London, there's nothing else but this. If you get up and walk out, as you walk out of here what will arise will be nothing arising as everything and it'll look like a staircase. So you don't need to go anywhere or know anything. Enlightenment is nothing to do with knowing everything, seeing everything, seeing what's happening in Africa, because this is everything. This is totally everything.

*But if I'm in Africa then Africa is everything.*

Yes, absolutely.

*And while I'm in Africa this doesn't exist.*

No, absolutely not. Your house doesn't exist, your lover doesn't exist ... have you got a lover? *(laughing)*

*So this is all there is?*

This is all there is and it doesn't matter what the mind thinks it can do about it. Wherever mind goes and whatever it does is only ever being appearing as this.

The whole of this manifestation is in one way promoting the paradox that you are a separate person sitting in a room with seventy or eighty other separate people. "I am something. He is something. Tom is something. So Tony Parsons is something." Whereas in reality this is simply nothing talking to nothing. Nothing is saying to nothing, "Come on, there is already nothing and everything."

*Experience of body-mind is no different than experience of thought?*

No, it's just what's happening. I have to say that when awakening apparently happens, one of the last things that drops away is a sense of location, because it's so ingrained in us that this is my body and I walk around. When I walk out of here that's what's seen. In a way that's the last thing that drops away. The realisation that this body is just body. It's not anyone's body. It's not owned.

*I always think about my childhood and maybe it's the first ever location that is there ... this is there and this is me, this is you ...*

And then a very powerful part of that is seeking pleasure and avoiding pain. So after separation, because there's already a longing, we seek pleasure and avoid pain, so we start becoming "business" people. We smile at our mother naturally and she smiles back and we like it so we go on doing it.

○  ○  ○

*Is there any point in oneness knowing oneness?*

Well oneness doesn't need to know anything. There is only oneness. There's not an action. All there is is this. It's totally action-less. And in it arises apparent action. But in the dream of being a separate individual, everything still arises uniquely because there is only that.

So in that dream, everything is totally, uniquely for that. In liberation, in the realisation of oneness, there is still that uniqueness. The difference is that there's no-one in there that that's happening to. It just is apparently happening. It is no thing arising as uniqueness. It's totally incomprehensible, unknowing isness without a knower.

It can never be understood that in liberation, when there is no-one, when the whole separation has dropped away, there is still the unique duality that appears to be arising. But it is then completely seen through as a play of being.

○  ○  ○

*So, sometimes you talk about vertical time as opposed to linear time.*

No, not vertical time. Verticality.

*Verticality. So is that when that shift, whatever it is, sort of apparently happens? Is that the ending of the story?*

It is seeing that there is only this which is time-less, and it's also enjoying the story of time but seeing through the story, seeing that the story is totally meaningless and has no relevance or power any more. It only apparently happens in time, that's what it is.

*But it is seen by ...?*

The story is seen as nothing being everything. I really wouldn't try to understand this.

*So it'd be true to say, and I think you've said it several times, probably on this retreat, that in ordinary life there is actually a lot of ordinary seeing, including thoughts, and that's just normal. We all do it without realising it. And then this sort of psychology, I sense, comes in as a veil claiming ownership through the habit of prescriptive living.*

Yes. So then when awakening happens it will report, "Oh, it's what has always been there."

*Exactly.*

So actually there is only beingness. In the whole of this appearance there is only what is. There's only this happening. It's inescapable. It's the all and everything.

*Somehow the psychology I sense that comes up and says "I", it sort of blocks the seeing of itself because it's so fine it covers the ...*

Yes. So it's the open secret.

*Exactly, yes.*

It's the secret all the time there is someone there that's trying to work it out. Then it stays secret. And it's only when there's nobody looking for it that it becomes open and apparent.

*It's like eternity isn't it?*

It is eternity.

*Yet when we talk, people say "I was enlightened yesterday," but there was never a yesterday to be enlightened in.*

No. And there was no-one to be enlightened.

*It's so gentle, isn't it?*

Gentle, yes.

*Gently amazing.*

Yes. Yes it is.

*I think the mind just doesn't get that.*

No, no.

*It's ungraspable.*

That's one thing that really struck me after the initial awakening, when there was no-one there and then someone came back to report on it. I was interested in Christianity at the time and I didn't understand this stupid idea that you could sin, and then you were forgiven. I suddenly saw that the real meaning in forgiveness is that there's absolutely no-one and nothing to forgive. It doesn't matter how many times you seem to get it wrong or whatever you do, or whatever you

37

don't do. It doesn't matter how much you seek or do not seek. There is only being this. It is unconditional love.

*Did you feel a sense of relief?*

Well it was just a wonder. The real meaning or quality behind the ideas that we have makes an absolute nonsense of the religious dogmas and the idea of original sin ...

*Feels like part of the gentleness is a very deep kind of humour.*

Yes, absolutely. There's a real, real, deep humour in all of this. I mean in a way it's a cosmic joke. It is *the* cosmic joke. It's the best joke in town.

*The only joke in town.*

The only joke, yes. In another way you could very simply say aliveness is all there is. And aliveness is felt through the five senses and also through the sixth and seventh senses of feelings arising and thoughts happening. All of that is pure aliveness. There is nothing other than aliveness. That is all there is.

And what's amazing about it is that everybody in this room is pure aliveness. What's sitting here is just simply, utterly aliveness. And that's the beginning and the end of it all. There isn't any need to say any more than that. Thank you.

# 3

The Sanskrit word Advaita points to something which can't be spoken of. Although we will be doing a lot of speaking, we can never ever describe what we are trying to talk about. Nor can it be understood or known.

The word Advaita also points to the futility of the idea that there is something separate from something else called oneness. So we won't be talking about reaching a state – we won't be here to try and find states of bliss or stillness or silence, or even awareness. No amount of self-enquiry will bring the seeker to that which already is. So, we won't be here looking for anything because there is nothing to find and nothing to get.

What we are talking about is so obvious that it is utterly obscure and it's so open that it is utterly secret. All the time there is someone trying to get it, it stays hidden. All the time we look for it, it just isn't seen. It can't be attained, it can't be lost, it can't be taught, it can't be given and it can't be taken away.

It can't be talked about or grasped because it is already nothing and everything. It is not only the biggest thing in this room, it is the only thing in this room – it's the only arising in this room. It's all that's happening in this room. And within it – within what we seek – is us seeking it. And so the seeking of being is also being seeking. And all the time that we believe we are separate from it or experience that we are separate from it – then we are inevitably seeking it.

The seeker can only function in moving to find what it dreams it has lost. And it is moving to find something that is utterly still. The clock's ticking and seeking is moving in time to anticipate finding something that is timeless and still.

What we are talking about has nothing to do with you or me – absolutely nothing to do with you or me. It has nothing to do with personal experience. You are not going to get this, nobody has ever got this, because it has to do with there being nobody. I haven't got it. I don't know anything you don't know – I haven't got something you don't have, but something has been lost.

This is about loss, this is about a total loss. And it's a loss of something that we have grown up to believe in – we have grown up to believe that we are individuals – that we are separate individuals with free will and choice and we can do something to make our lives work in the world, and in some way or other the mind seeks to help us do that. But some of us are more sensitive to the idea that life isn't just about success or about being rich and all of that.

And so we look in religion or we look in therapy or meditation or we look in self-enquiry – we look in the school of enlightenment for that which will bring us to some sort of wholeness. We know that there is something that isn't whole. This isn't it, this isn't quite it. It is slightly out of line – there is something else. Is it enlightenment?

And the mind will then paint a picture of what enlightenment is like. Enlightenment is bliss, omni-presence, omni-power, everybody loves you, you love everyone and you walk around in this beautiful pink haze. *(laughter)* People come to you and they say, "I hear you are enlightened?" and you say, "Yes." *(laughter)* "Well, would you come and speak to some of my friends?", and you say, "Yes, OK ..." And you go and there are a few friends and you tell them about how you have become enlightened and they love that – that sounds good – and they look at you and you are sort of very quiet and obviously completely together and in bliss. But they want to be like you and their friends want to be like you so they get more friends and they come and you get more people in the room and in the end it has to be a bigger room and the crowds get bigger. And then you say to your friend, "Well you know, I am down here on this level – maybe I ought to have a platform, maybe a bigger seat so the people can see me."

You know, we have got this idea – the mind has an idea of what enlightenment is like; it's the lottery, it's the spiritual lottery. It's the biggest lottery that you can win. It's better than winning 100 million pounds because you have got everything, you are just there, you are totally safe, you have got bliss and everything is wonderful.

And that is the difficulty, because of course, actually, enlightenment is nothing like that. Enlightenment, liberation, is totally, utterly ordinary. It is not wonderful. It's not blissful, it is not the answer to everything. Life goes on. It goes on just as it did before. But the difference in liberation is the dropping away of any sense that there is anyone that life is happening to. Liberation is absence, liberation is loss – the loss of separation. And in that loss, the emptiness is filled.

That emptiness is also fullness. In nothing – when there is nothing – everything fills nothing.

Ask any question – it doesn't matter what question you ask. If a question arises it is there to arise and meet nothing and be answered by nothing. The mind can never get anywhere with this.

This is totally simple, utterly simple and very difficult. It is very simple because it is totally obvious, and it is difficult because it is frightening to the individual – the sense of losing individuality is a frightening idea to the individual.

○ ○ ○

*You were saying yesterday that the very seeking prevents the seeing – I am paraphrasing – it's just such a brilliant game of appearances and deflection of attention in a way and it just helps to give an understanding of how it is all from the same font.*

It's the same font, yes. One bit of it doesn't want to be the same – or thinks it isn't the same font.

*But that's just all the play – or what is called "the divine play of ... "*

It's absolutely the divine play of being. And being isn't the slightest bit interested in the idea of anybody seeing this or not, because there is nothing other than being ... and non-realisation is also being.

So being suffers, being laughs, being searches, being finds, being doesn't find. There isn't anything other than that. And of course all of that is totally immaculately whole – there is only that so that is all there is. But in that wholeness there is something that thinks it isn't wholeness, which is also being, being separate.

Being has no requirements. But what arises within being is an apparent need and requirement to find that there is no need and requirement.

*And the mystery of that is just inscrutable – it's just a mystery.*

And the search for that is reflected in the world that we live in because everything we do is a search for that. All religion, all apparent personal endeavour, is simply a seeking for this unknowing.

*A resolution of attention, of feeling separate?*

It is a search for not being separate. The seeker cannot see this, because this is timeless being – this is the eternal isness which is out of time, out of space, out of being achievable. So what we are trying to achieve can't be achieved because it is already all there is.

*It's kind of hard to accept – something I have a hard time accepting is that the spiritual search is no better, no higher, no more refined than a search for money, sex, power or whatever.*

Absolutely. All desire is ultimately the search to come home. And what is strange about this paradox, this mystery, is that everything that is being done – all seeking, all reaching out, all personal endeavour, all building of churches and empires – is being-ness. It is pure aliveness. It's an amazingly strange paradox.

*In some ancient Vedic text, or something like that, is there anything said about how that is, or about the why? I mean I know the* Bhagavad Gita *says just, it's an experiment ...*

No, there is no why and there is no experiment and no choice. The basis of traditional argument is that oneness chose to become two, and if oneness made a choice to become two, it could make a choice to become one again. It's a fairy story based on the illusion of time, cause and effect.

Nothing is ever chosen. The whole dream of choice and motivation is that there is something in time that can move forward with intention from a place called "twoness" to a place called "oneness". There never has been anything but being, and this is the eternal nothing and everything. It isn't going anywhere and it's never been anywhere. There is no anywhere. There is no time or space except in the appearance. There is nothing but this, and this is nothing happening.

*And I see now that that question arises from the sepa-*
*rate point of view so it is inherently unanswerable in a*
*way. It is just an unanswerable question, but that is only*
*because it is from the standpoint of separateness. Because*
*in the glimpses of wholeness there is no question. There is*
*no question at all. There is just an absence of any need to*
*know anything because it just is. So then that question is*
*just a loop that arises.*

Yes, it is a loop and you are absolutely right, separation engenders the question "why" and the searching.
And as you say, when there is no-one there is no loop
and there won't be any questions. There is no question
and there are no answers. There is no knower and no
known ... and so there is no-one to ask why.

*But it is the most enticing question within that point*
*of view.*

Oh yes, it is, and being in separation loves asking
why. And that fascination has generated religion. The
question "why" in the seeker has generated Christianity, Buddhism, and everything else that you could call
a teaching of becoming that inevitably is based on the
fundamental misconception that there is a separate
individual with choice and volition to follow a path,
to be motivated to move from one state to another,
better state, to seek and find the answer that has no
question.

*And it is also an insistence from the separate point of*
*view to want the answer – it is an insistence of the very*
*existence of the separate point of view. But if I exist, I*
*should be able to have an answer about this because I can*

*think this, I can experience this – it is kind of an insistence of "I EXIST".*

Absolutely – totally. The question in mind is the insistence that I am a separate individual and want an answer; and demand, and have the right, to have an answer. The difference between here and elsewhere is that the response to the questions is not feeding the seeking mind. The mind continuously meets a pointing towards that which it cannot comprehend. That is how the questioning dries up and then there is nothing left.

The other very powerful element of seeking an answer is the experience of unworthiness, because the feeling of separation is a feeling of being rejected from wholeness. So immediately a huge sense of unworthiness arises and of course most religions, most 'isms', appeal directly to that sense of unworthiness. So that is another powerful element of the search because religions and teachings of becoming are teaching us how to overcome our dreamt unworthiness which is based on fallacy.

It is such a powerful message – "Yes I am unworthy, I feel unworthy. There is something wrong. So it must be me that did it wrong. Can you teach me how to do it right?"

○ ○ ○

*Tony, can I ask you … in this issue of time, there are occasions, in my experience, when it's very clear that this is this. But at other times you go, for example, and look in a churchyard and see an old tombstone which is of a different time.*

It reports to you a different time but it is still only this … what is apparently happening.

*Yes, and so it appears to be something that happened before and sometimes I see past that confusion and sometimes I don't. I was just wondering if you could say something about it.*

Well, all the time that there is still a separate entity then what is seen appears as a story. If you are looking at a gravestone, "Bill Daniels - Died in 1917", this is a story about someone else in your story.

*So there was no Bill Daniels?*

Oh no.

*So Tony, when you say that this is all nothing, then these appearances, the wall and apparent characters – it's all just an illusion?*

I think the word "illusion" is a bit misleading. It's nothing appearing as something. It's both real and unreal. It's nothing appearing as a wall and it has all the apparatus of seeming real. This is nothing appearing as bodies. That's why in liberation it is seen that everything is both something and nothing. So everything is seen as it is, there is no veil. The veil is the veil of thinking that everything else is also only another separate something.

*Are you saying that there is always an appearance of some sort or another. So even in …*

No there isn't. There is no always.

*There isn't an appearance?*

There is and there isn't. But there is no always. What the dream of separation brings with it is the belief in the reality of time, and story, a before and after and a conviction that there is an always.

*So, for example, in deep sleep, isn't that another phenomenon in itself?*

All there is is nothing being everything and so everything is nothing. This can never be comprehended. It is essentially, by its very nature, unknowable.

Deep sleep is being no-thing. Phenomena arise in being-ness or nothing – which is the same thing. So in deep sleep nothing seems to arise; however, it is nothing and everything, emptiness and fullness.

*But it's not a question of one or the other?*

There is no-one or other, except in the dream of separation. It's only that the everything, the fullness, isn't appearing to be sitting in a room wearing brown jackets and blue jumpers. It is seemingly totally still ... unmoving. This is a story being described right now ... when the thing wakes up within which that no-thing seems to be, then nothing begins to move around and appears to be something and drink coffee. What's apparently happening right now is deep sleep. This is emptiness appearing to be aliveness happening.

*It's a great relief when you say that nothing really happens because we spend our whole lives trying to make something out of nothing and you think, "Oh, thank God for that!" You know, it's been confirmed here that in everything you are trying desperately to make happen you are always aware that it never actually quite gets there.*

No it never will, because of course nobody is doing anything, they only believe that they are making things happen and there is somewhere to get to. It is like trying to write on water.

○ ○ ○

*Tony, yesterday evening you introduced the idea of self-consciousness.*

Yes.

*Well, what is self-consciousness?*

Self-consciousness is uniquely something that the human being adopts or takes on board at a very early age. There is nothing and then something arises called "being separate", if you like, or self-consciousness. "I am conscious that I am a separate self." It is the story of the Garden of Eden; you eat the apple of "self consciousness" – knowledge of self. Being arises and is apparently separate and then self-consciousness arises ... but only apparently.

*It is very powerful, because I realise that everything is being referred to by this self-consciousness.*

Oh, it seems so. But it only seems meaningful and important to the apparent "me" which adds itself to being and dreams or believes it is now in a story about "me".

*It is not only a story, it is even more than a story.*

It is only a story. Let's say, after a year of being-ness, nothing but being ... no story, and suddenly, *(claps hands)* the story starts. "This is the story of Tony Parsons, or Bill or Henry", in time, in space, growing up with a family. "I am an individual, my mother and father are individuals, my priest, my teacher, my boss, my girlfriend and my wife are all individuals and we are all together in a world in which we are separate and we have free will and choice to do something. Because of course this place I now find myself in must have meaning. It's all got to have a meaning! *(laughter)* This feeling of disquiet, this feeling of loss must mean something. It means that I get married and have a lovely job and three kids and it is all wonderful. Or I become a Christian and find the Kingdom of Heaven." It's all got to have meaning because it is a story with a beginning and end ... apparently.

*But it's also spontaneous, this self-consciousness?*

Apparently, yes. No-one is doing it, at any level, nobody is doing it. It is just intelligent energy. There is only energy appearing as a story.

*Apparently moving.*

Yes, there is nothing out there directing it, there is nothing. There just is absolutely only energy appearing as this. There is no will, there is no greater will. There is no choice, there is no choice of any kind.

*So self-consciousness is another word for being ...*

Yes, for being separate.

*I think there's nothing wrong with self-consciousness ...*

No! Of course, in being there is nothing wrong with anything. How could there be in unicity?

*Because the flower flowers and human beings ...*

Well flowers aren't self-conscious. I haven't come across a self-conscious flower. But what arises in that self-conscious story is the idea that there is something right and wrong. Because the moment that we become separate we think it is wrong, and we are "wrong". The moment we become separate apparent dualism arises. "Is there somewhere else called paradise or wholeness? Why am I not in wholeness? There is something wrong and if there is something wrong then there must be something right. So I have got to find something right to make the wrong right. So I am going to become a Buddhist or whatever you like." The minute that is there then all the drama of good and evil breaks loose. You have got cause and effect, right and wrong, karma and reincarnation, time, space, separation, path – all those things that reinforce the really important idea that I am an individual and there is somewhere that is better than this. If you look at all religions they are about somewhere that is better than this. They are all totally denying that this is it.

○  ○  ○

*Tony, the mind just can't see it anyway.*

No, the mind can't see it because the mind is simply being mind-ing and the function of the mind is to divide and move forward or backwards. It only moves, so it can't comprehend stillness.

*But there is a definite difference between the seeing of what is and then the mind coming back and trying to explain it.*

It's the story of the man in the desert finding truth and then God saying to the Devil, "Man has found the truth now, what are you going to do about that?" And the Devil says, "Well, I am going to help him organise it." So there is a seeing of this, the mind comes in and tries to turn it into something it can try to deal with.

*And then there is a sort of memory somewhere of what was seen. Is that mind?*

It is an attempt to remember that which is boundless and unknowable. The words can never express this. The mind can only conceptualise this.

*Well it's like it comes in ...*

It can't possible know stillness because it is stillness moving.

*Exactly, yes ... yeah. (laughs) It's just so close, I mean it's just here.*

In a sense the moment you start thinking about it being close then you are back into thinking it is another something, another object. It's this. It's aliveness. And in a way that is the nearest you can get to it. There is nothing but aliveness which is beingness. It is so directly this, it is not recognisable by anything else!

*And when this is apparent, or there is this recognition*

*of all there is, that's not the mind telling me ...*

Well it can be. The mind can tell you about al. ......
is. And there are people that will just sit there and say
to you, "All there is is being. There is no-one. All there
is, is what's arising." So it can be conceptualised but
actually this is totally felt. It is actually indescribably
lived-in. You can't describe it. It is cogently, vibrantly
alive.

*Alive, yes, aliveness. Because I am quite concerned
that the mind always comes back.*

But in the end it is realised that the mind is just
beingness, mind-ing. It is totally at home – it's just
another thing. It's really the seventh sense. There are
the five senses, the sixth sense of feelings – and the
seventh sense is thinking. So thinking is the seventh
sense. It is not the enemy.

*Yes, it's OK.*

And then it takes its place. It has no power any
more, it is just seen as another thing that is happening,
apparently. It is not the enemy of being.

*It is so second nature to personalise everything.*

It seems to be. It's very hypnotic.

*Yes, it's like a hypnotism ... amazing.*

The hypnotic dream that everything is happening
to "me" is very powerful and it is the basic belief of
most people. That's why this message is a total revolution because it topples everything. Everything that we
believe in collapses and there is nothing left.

*But there is a powerful pull to draw you back in.*

Because it is about self-survival. We have to survive so we go on playing the game of being individuals calculating everything. We don't see everything, we see what we think of as something else and what we could do about it and whether it is desirable or whether it's a threat. We don't see anything except through a veil of self-survival.

*Or even the identity of opinions, it is so intoxicating to have an opinion and to express it in a discussion or make a point.*

To make ourselves feel better about us – to maintain or reinforce a sense of personal worth.

*Incredible.*

It is beingness playing out the apparent story

○  ○  ○

*You say that when we die that we will be reunited with ...*

No, no, no. How can there be re-unification when there is nothing dis-united?

*But we don't feel this unity?*

Whilst we only dream being a part of the unity, this is separation. When the dream is awoken from, there is only unity. There is nothing that feels, knows or is aware.

*So what happens then?*

There is no then as there is no now or before now.

All there is is nothing *appearing* to happen within something else which is *appearing* as time.

*There is no difference? There is no difference between now and at my point of death?*

Who is going to die? There is no-one who is born or who dies. There is no difference between this and your point of death but you think there is a difference. You think you are sitting there. You think you are what has happened and what will happen ... this is the nature of the hypnotic dream of separation.

*Yes, sure. So this absolute nothing is an energy which we could call "love"?*

Well this absolute nothing is nothing and everything. This absolute nothing is emptiness and fullness.

*Is this love?*

You could say the nature of being nothing and everything is stillness, silence, the uncaused, unrelated, impersonal unconditional love, but that's just words trying to describe the indescribable.

*Um, the nothing that we were – well the nothing that is – appears to have awareness now.*

Awareness, knowing, seeing, hearing is nothing arising as those apparent phenomena within the wholeness.

*And would that awareness that is a part of nothing still be there at death?*

You see, you are still applying time to the eternal isness. Awareness, like a consciousness of time or being separate is simply a personal experience. It is simply what is apparently happening in manifestation ... in the story.

*So it is simply part of consciousness?*

Yes, the awareness is just another thing that is happening, apparently. That is my sense of the word "awareness". Some people think that awareness is being-ness, but I think that's very misleading because the whole sense of awareness requires something for it to be aware of. So if there is awareness there is something else that it needs to be aware of. There is still an activity which requires this and that.

*Well like me, the energy that is expressing itself...*

It's not expressing itself – we are back to a deep mystery. There is only nothing and awareness is nothing arising as awareness.

*But did you not say that everything is energy?*

Yes, but in answering your question I am saying that everything is just pure energy and awareness is apparently happening within it.

*And the intelligent energy, could that not be awareness?*

Awareness would arise in that, but being wouldn't need to be aware because it is already everything.

# 4

So this is not a message about you or me or anyone getting anything. This is about the realisation that there's nothing to get ... that what has been sought has never been lost.

This isn't about seeking or not seeking; it's beyond the concepts of Advaita and non-dualism and beyond the idea of reaching states of awareness or mindfulness. There's no goal. There's nothing on offer. This is totally beyond knowing. So, this is the worst place for the individual to be because there's nothing available to hope for.

This is really a description – a sharing together of a description of something that is beyond attainment, something that can't be lost and also can't be grasped or gained.

All the time there's separation there's a sense of loss, there's a sense of a feeling that there's something that isn't whole. And so the seeker attempts to fill that void, fill it with something – whatever. And some look to something called "enlightenment" because it is felt that enlightenment might be the thing that will fill this sense of loss; it could be the answer to some secret that we don't quite get.

And it sounds, when we read about enlightenment, as though somebody else has found the secret. But nobody's found the secret.

There's no such thing as an enlightened person. It's a complete misconception. But the difficulty is that being seekers, the energy of seeking pushes us into being attracted to the idea that somebody else has found something that we can find, because we grow up believing that effort brings results. So, if effort brings results, and we've heard of something called enlightenment or liberation, we can make the effort and then we can become liberated or enlightened ... like this guy up the road we've heard about, or that woman that's giving satsangs. They have got something that I want. If I go there I will learn how to get it.

In the dream there's still an idea that enlightenment or liberation is something that's attainable. And so there are teachings that reinforce the idea that you are an individual that has choice, so now you, as an individual, can choose to self-enquire or to meditate, or whatever else, and eventually you could become enlightened.

You can go all over the world and find teachings offering something to get. It is rare, however, to find an uncompromising communication that offers nothing at all to the seeker.

This aliveness is nothing being everything. It's just

life happening. It's not happening to anyone. There's a whole set of experiences happening here and they're happening in emptiness ... they're happening in free fall. They're just what's happening. All there is is life. All there is is beingness. There isn't anyone that ever has or does not have it. There's nobody that has life and somebody else doesn't have life. There just is life being life.

This message is so simple it totally confounds the mind. This message is too simple. Already your mind's saying, "Yes, but come on ... what about the levels of enlightenment and what about my emotional blocks, and what about my chakras, they're not all fully open? What about my stillness – I'm not really still yet, and what about my ego? Somebody told me I still have an ego ... it's a bit reduced but it's still there." *(laughing)*

But all of that, all of those ideas are adopted lessons about how it should be. The ego is what's happening. The ego is just being ego. Thinking is just being thinking. There is only being. There is just being. There's nothing else. There's nobody that's running that. There's no destiny, there's no God, there's no plan, there's no script, there's nowhere to go because there is only timeless being. Being is totally whole just being. And it is alive and fleshy and sexy and juicy and immediately this; it's not some concept about 'there's no-one here'. It's not some concept about 'there's nowhere to go'. It is the aliveness that's in that body right now. There is pure beingness, pure aliveness. That's it. End of story. You can all go home now ... *(laughing)* as long as you've paid. *(laughing)*

59

Really it is simply that. So there is no-one, there is no choice. There is no choice at any level. Oneness didn't choose to become two. There is just oneness. All there is in this room is oneness being alive with nobody doing it. Is anybody doing breathing? Is anybody doing blood circulation? Is anybody really doing anything? No. There is just apparent doing. Apparent life in unknowingness.

So, we can talk together and although there will be questions, there aren't actually any answers. There is no answer to life because life is its own answer *(claps hands)*. It's happening already. It's this. You never lost it. That's the amazing thing about awakening. When awakening apparently happens people say, "It's amazing because the thing I was looking for has never left me. It's the one thing that never comes and never goes – the one constant that can't be known or held onto." And the one constant is being. You could get up and walk out right now and there's just being walking out. You can never escape being. All there is, is being.

This has nothing to do with me or you. I don't have anything. You don't have anything.

○ ○ ○

*I feel very happy to be here. I want to address the topic of being. Yesterday I learned a very important lesson. I was on my way home and I thought, "Oh I'm so much looking forward to being at home," and I realised that I was actually tearing myself in two because I was saying by implication that my state in travelling was actually less than this nirvana of simply this.*

*And I said, "Hang on, Robert, it's you here, stop mort-gaging yourself for some future event, it's actually OK to be on the train".*

Yes. But *you* didn't do that, it just happened. And looking forward is also beingness.

*It just happened?*

The difficulty for the seeker is that they think they have to do something about their state or be in another state that frees them from the state they think they're in.

*But you're a left brain torturer aren't you?*

Oh, am I? *(laughing)*

*Of course you are.*

Oh right, I'm a left brain torturer. *(laughing)*

So in Amsterdam I'm "the Terminator". And here I'm the "left brain torturer". *(laughing)*

*You know you said there's just awareness?*

No, there's just being. Awareness happens, or doesn't happen, in being.

*There's just being. And you were talking about aware-ness as a sense.*

Well my sense of awareness is that it's a transient state, or it's a place you can be in and out of. It's still in the story.

*Because I was just thinking that – when you were*

61

*standing there – I was aware of your left side. I'm also aware that my shoulder's a bit tense but nobody else in the room is aware of it.*

No.

*So it's as if we all have separate awareness.*

Well yes, that seems to be so, and what I'm suggesting is that all these things you've just described are something that's simply happening. It's being tight shoulders or being Tony Parsons' left side. It doesn't need awareness for it to be, but the seeker thinks it does.

*But what's happening here is slightly different to what's happening there.*

What's also being suggested is that there isn't a "here" and "there". It seems to the apparent entity that there is a location here and it seems as though there's a "here" and a "there". There isn't a "here" and a "there" and those tight shoulders are simply being tight shoulders just as being this left side is being left side. It's all only beingness.

*But it's all lots of little different bits of information.*

Yes it certainly seems different, but it is oneness being everything and therefore appearing to be different. All of it is simply oneness arising. All of it is simply being.

*What do we do with all the bits of information coming at us all the time?*

Nothing.

*Nothing?* (laughing)

There is no-one that can do anything and there is nothing that needs to be done or known! There never has been anyone to do anything. The whole misconception that keeps us firmly in the sense of being separate is the idea that we can do anything or the idea that we need to do anything. Why do we need to do anything? There is just what's happening. It is all immaculately complete and without need.

*So what should we be aware of then?*

Nothing. *(laughing)* Here you go again with the obligation of having to be aware, which is a transitory state. There just is what's happening. The idea of being aware of something is a trap. Awareness needs another and is still in the story of dualism ... there is no other.

*But what's happening changes; it changes from second to second. That's not constant.*

Yes. It certainly appears to change, but everything only seems to change or be different or apart from everything else. All of what happens is being apparently happening.

*So where's the constant?*

The constant is being, and it is nowhere and everywhere. What's happening is being arising and moving around. And beingness is all there is.

*And where am I in relation to what's happening?*

You aren't. There is no-one. There is no relationship.

All there is is being and the idea of a "me" arises in being.

*Hmm-mm.* (laughing) *Well what's the value of knowing that?*

None at all. There's absolutely nothing on offer here. There's no value, nothing is on offer. The most amazing thing that could arise from this is nothing. If you go out of here with something, then you're still someone with something. "I now have this. This is mine to do something with." If there's a real hearing of this it will be seen that there is nothing to get or know. There will just be apparently what's happening.

There's nowhere to go. There's no goal. There's no carrot. There's no prize. All there is is this. But the difference between there just being what's happening and the sense that it's happening to you is immeasurable.

○ ○ ○

*Is there anything I can do about coming to that level of awareness or being or whatever?*

There isn't, not because there is someone who can't do anything but because there is no-one and there is no level to get to! In that absence there are no other levels. There is only nothing and everything.

What can apparently happen is the sudden realisation that already all there is is being. And in reality, that's all there is. All there is in this room is being and also what's arising is the idea that there isn't only being.

But that idea that there isn't only being is also being.

*Yes, but there's nothing for me to do.*

But that would imply there's someone there that can do nothing. That's not what is being said. There isn't anyone sitting there. All there is is life happening. And there's nothing there that has ever done anything or will ever do anything. The doing is an appearance of doing.

*So how is it that you came to this level of understanding?*

I didn't. That's the whole point. I didn't. Nobody ever has. It isn't a level of understanding ... it is unknowing.

*But do you still experience yourself as an individual in that you've decided to come and give a talk and you're explaining something to us because we want something? Or is this just happening?*

This is only what's happening. There is no individual experience here and there is no intent or agenda ... except in the dream of "you" as someone who wants something. That desire will never be satisfied here because it is recognised that there is no-one who needs help. So you want something but you won't get it.

*So you don't know in advance what's going to be next?*

No, and neither do you. You only want to believe that you can know what's going to happen next so that you can feel in control. It's a dream called "me knowing". *(laughing)*

*I think I do.*

Yes, that's the thing, we think we can anticipate. We grow up in a world that's separate and we feel frightened about it so we try to control it. So what we do is we try to live in the known. We try to anticipate and find answers. But actually if we try to live in this known world it seems to become a bit dull. But the strange thing is that being is unknowable. What's being suggested here, and is actually happening, is totally unknowable. There is no-one in this room that has any idea what's going to happen next. (silence)

*It sounds such a simple message and yet it seems to be very difficult as well.*

Yes. So you can't get rid of yourself. All the time *you* try to get rid of *you*, you are getting bigger and bigger. It's very simple, but frightening for the apparent individual.

*Yes.*

But what's being suggested here is that strangely, when this is heard, something can apparently happen. Because this is not a conceptual thing – there's not somebody here trying to sell a concept or trying to sell a belief. There isn't anybody here trying to sell anything. Nothing is for sale.

Awakening is energetic ... you grow up in a contracted state, and there is simply an explosion into the boundless. I don't know anything. It's a sudden intuitive seeing that, *"Yes! This is all there is. This is it."* It is a remembering, a rediscovery of what already is.

*(laughing)*

*So why have a mind?*

Well there's nothing that can be done about that. *(laughing)*

There's no such thing as a mind. There's a thought and a thought and a thought ... and thinking likes to sit on the throne telling you that it'll get you there. It'll make you a lot of money or it'll get him to love you. It'll apparently do all sorts of things. It promises to help you with your life and it will also promise you disaster. It will tell you all those things. And the mind, thinking, is always about tomorrow. It's always going to happen tomorrow when you've meditated for long hours, or self-enquired or tried to fast or become celibate or renounce desire ... it's always later on, after this or that has happened, simply because thinking apparently only functions in time, in the story of me. It is always seeking the answer but there is no answer.

These days there's a lot of energy about self-enquiry. Who's making the tea? Who's driving your car? Who's sitting listening to Tony Parsons? Who am I? Who am I? Self-enquiry can offer you a special place within yourself that is detachment ... it is another spiritual lollipop. It's like *being here now*. People go and hear about being here now and they really work hard at being here now and it lasts sometimes for half an hour because it is simply another personal state within the story of me.

*Is awakening quite disorientating?*

It can vary. Sometimes strange energy seems to happen, sometimes nothing at all. People can wake up in the morning and it's all over. There's no-one. There's just this. It's very ordinary. This is totally ordinary and natural. What we do is impose something on it.

*So although it's totally ordinary it's so opposite to what has been held onto.*

Yes, it is. It's a total revolution. It's a revolution of 360 degrees.

*I think one of the main reasons I come to these meetings is this kind of yearning to be free of a sense of responsibility and the weight of that.*

Oh, right. That's something that you want. This communication is about something that's beyond the idea of what you want ... it's even beyond the idea of there being a *you* who wants to be free of responsibility.

*It sounds like what's being communicated is being without that weight of responsibility.*

The idea of being or not being responsible simply does not arise in liberation.

*So it sounds as if there's a state of being that doesn't involve that. You know, getting caught up in those sorts of situations.*

So, you mean it's a state that sounds better than the present one.

*Yes.*

Liberation is better for no-one. There isn't someone

there who's in a better state. There is no-one to be in a state.

*But the sense of wanting to be free from that?*

But there won't be any one that's free, there will only be freedom. There's no-one that needs to be free. There's no-one that needs liberation.

○  ○  ○

*Tony, this spiritual physiology of chakras and third eyes and auras, is that just a story or ...?*

Yes. It's the mind wanting to continue and therefore create as much complication as it can in order that becoming continues. It thrives within the promise of the idea that things will get better.

So, the whole idea of the person choosing to do some work on themselves is a fallacy born from the idea that there's such a thing as self-will or volition to bring about a state which is better than the present one.

*So there needs to be no concern about all that stuff?*

But who is not going to be concerned any longer? All the time there is the seeking energy there is a search for something better.

*So this means there is no point in doing anything?*

No, again, that's not it either. The ideas of "doing" and "there being a point" are part of the dream of separation. There is no-one who can do anything and there's nothing to be done. Everything is already complete.

*I want to make choice.*

Well you dream you are someone who can do that.

*I have to make the choice.*

Why would you have to make a choice?

*I don't know. It just happens.*

Ah! Absolutely, it just happens. But what you add to it is the idea that you are doing it.

*I thought that this was beingness just asking a question.*

Yes it is beingness just asking the question.

*But I had to make a choice.*

No, you didn't have to. There isn't anyone. Asking a question just happened.

*What did I do?*

There is no you.

*I thought I made a choice of speaking or not speaking.*

No, it just happened. The dreamer doesn't think, thinking happens ... thinking  arrives and we think that *we* are thinking. Thinking just happens and we dream we are choosing to act out of *our* thought.

*If I take my ego and completely dissolve into awareness or something, what would I do next?*

*(Laughing)* I love it so much. It's always *your* ego, *your* awareness ... you are such a rich man. There is no-one. Who's ever owned an ego?

*Well I have an ego.*

Oh, you do? So you have some ownership. Do you have a house? A flat? Maybe a flat. So do you own quite a small ego or is it semi-detached? There is no-one. No-one has an ego. This is about freedom from the idea of owning. Wouldn't it be lovely to just drop all these little bags called "ego", "free will" and "desire", and drop the person that owns them? Let them just be there. Let them just be what happens. Enjoy the utter nakedness of isness.

*And what would you be left with?*

You'd be left with nothing, but the strange thing is you've never had anything anyway. You only dream you do. The idea that you're a separate person arises and then you think you own something. It's a dream. It's a dream called "being separate and owning things". Owning things makes you feel real. When all that's left is nothing then it is filled with everything. Liberation is absolute poverty and absolute abundance.

○  ○  ○

*A lot of the time I feel I hang on to such a dream because I'm afraid of the consequences of letting go of it. So there's sort of a thought process, the thoughts that seem to constantly go on. It feels like it's something working something out; you know, the constant chatter.*

Absolutely. It's the mind protecting itself and trying to get there. But the ignorance is that it thinks that there's somewhere to get to. That's the whole seeking function ... something separate, you, and there's somewhere to get to. There's an approach you know, people call it "the Advaita approach". How can there be an Advaita approach? Advaita means oneness, or not two, or being. How can there be an approach to being? How can there be an approach to that which already is? Approach is being. There's no-one that can approach. All there is is beingness.

*Including the feeling that you need to do something about it?*

Yes, even that feeling is being feeling the need to do something in order to be. Approaching is being apparently approaching.

○　○　○

*Can you explain "nothing to forgive" because I've always thought that if you forgive everybody for everything then something often happens that helps.*

What I'm saying is that no-one's ever done anything and nothing's happening, so there's nothing to forgive. The whole idea that there's something to forgive presumes a relationship or a subject and an object. I am the subject, this other thing is an object that's done something to me and I can now forgive that and that will make me feel good. So the whole idea of being able to forgive somebody is the whole reinforcement of the idea of separation, of making things better ... of doing a deal.

*So if everybody did what you're suggesting ...*

That's the whole point. There is nobody to do anything or forgive anyone, except in the dream story.

*Right. And if it was possible?*

Now you're off again on another story – if you want to play games you can go ahead and do that. I'm not interested.

*I'm just wondering what the world would be like?*

The apparent world would be exactly like this. It is already complete.

It is actually all there is, including the idea that it isn't, including the idea that you are someone that can do something to me and I should forgive you for it. All of that is a story in the dream about there being separation and about making it a better world. If we all forgave each other it would be a better world. It's the dream of the need for something better.

First of all there's no-one who can forgive anybody and also these ideas are all based on the misconception that there is anything at fault or something wrong that needs putting right. I don't know if you've noticed but it seems for thousands and thousands of years of story we appear to have put a huge amount of energy into making the world a better place. How do you think it's going so far?

○   ○   ○

*Tony, if individuality is a dream, is life itself a dream?*

Well it is being arising as apparent life. So it's nothing arising as something. So all of this is simply being arising as apparently something happening. Separation is the dream that includes the idea of meaning, path and self-consciousness.

*OK.*

This manifestation is both real and unreal.

*I have a problem with this arising thing.*

Why?

*Because surely arising isn't being?*

Yes, what is apparently arising is absolutely being. It looks as though it's moving in time but it's absolute stillness moving, absolute silence sounding – this voice is silence, this clapping is one hand clapping.

*Yeah, but if something's arising then there's a gap, there's a time gap. You're anticipating something and it isn't being. All these non-dualists, including you, say there is no time.*

I'm not a non-dualist. And your anticipation of something is being *apparently* anticipating. And the gap is being *apparently* gapping! It's all there is ... there is no other.

*But this arising thing seems to put whatever this being thing is into the future.*

No. Everything *appears* to be arising in time. There is no time, there is no arising, it's only an appearance. The idea of a future is being *appearing* with an idea, in this, about the future.

*OK. It's not being?*

Yes it is absolutely being. Of course it's being, appearing to move, in seeming time, to somewhere. It's being appearing to have a purpose, "I have a goal to make the world a better place." All of that is simply being. It is a metaphor, a parable, a seeming reality.

*I notice on the timetable you've got a talk tomorrow at 2pm, but if you can't choose and you can't influence and if there's no time there can't be tomorrow, so how's it going to happen at all?*

It may apparently happen or, of course, it may not apparently happen. It doesn't happen at 2pm tomorrow. There is no 2pm tomorrow. But strangely enough at 2pm tomorrow it will seem to be happening at 2pm. *(laughing)*

*So is that your being? You're not influencing or choosing?*

There is no-one. There is no-one that owns a being. All there is is being. This is nothing being everything including the idea of separation and story and time. Within that being, planning and influence *apparently* arise.

*In some way things happen.*

It's an appearance. It's a hologram.

*So, I fear that what we have will fall apart if we give up running our lives.*

What you are saying perfectly expresses the power of hypnotic dreaming. That idea is based on a total misconception because actually we've never run our lives. Nobody runs their lives. You've never been in control. There is no-one. This is a very frightening message for those that believe and experience the idea of individual control.

*So it's going to happen anyway.*

Well, it's *apparently* happening. All that you add onto it is the idea that it's happening to you and you're in control of it. The idea that you're in control of it is a dream called separation. It's a fallacy.

○　○　○

*Sometimes I'm sure you've spoken in the past about certain things that apparent seekers do that perpetuate the sense of seeking.*

All action that comes out of the seeker perpetuates the dream of separation, because the seeker's only function is to find that which it longs for, and it thinks it can only find that in movement, in going forward, whereas actually what it's looking for is already being this. The inability to find oneness fuels the sense of separation.

*Are there conditions where it's more likely to be realised than other conditions?*

No, there aren't any conditions where it's more likely to be realised. It is already this. You could be drunk or sitting in a cave eating rice, it doesn't matter, because this apparent shift has absolutely nothing to do with the individual or their apparent action or state.

*So the idea of coming together for the sake of hearing this ...*

Has no relevance at all because that's all based on the idea that there has to be a circumstance. There are no circumstances because already all there is is this. Every apparent circumstance is this. It's the mind that devises the idea that there should be a certain circumstance, then the story can continue and survival is ensured.

*You know how you described the kind of state when an apparent person does come to this awareness and everything's changed and turned on its head. But is there a sort of halfway house or a sliding scale of degrees of awareness, or is it all or nothing?*

It is directly seen or not seen. For me, awareness is still a state in the story; there aren't states of being. There is only being and states arise in being including the state of awareness or the state of confusion. There is no such thing as half oneness.

*So, to come to the realisation and the recognition of what's what – I'm trying to ascertain whether you can sort of be nearly there?*

No, you can't be nearly being. There is only being. And somebody who is working hard on their chakras or meditating, or whatever you like, isn't someone who is getting near to being. There is only being and within that being can arise or appear to be someone who is working hard on their chakras or meditating to get somewhere.

*OK. In the darkness of night it's very black and there's no light, and in the middle of the day it's very bright, and at dawn and at dusk it's kind of twilight.*

Yes, this is the nature of story.

*Can one detect the onset of awareness through a kind of twilight?*

No. The whole world that we live in is a reflection of something that's beyond it, but the story seems to include time, the journey towards and away from life and death, light and dark. It's a parable. It's a parable about something that's beyond time, journey, paths and states of awareness and yet it includes them.

Again, being is not knowable.

○ ○ ○

*At the beginning of this meeting my mind went absolutely blank and free from the idea of getting anything, and then at the end there's a recognition that this message is very clear. So, something has happened.*

Yes. Clarity happens. But clarity isn't liberation. Clarity is something that someone can still have. There are plenty of people around these days who have been to these meetings and who have clarity about this. That has nothing to do with liberation.

*So there's no distinction between somebody who meets your words with utter confusion and somebody who has great clarity?*

No. Because this message is beyond the somebody or their understanding. Being is beyond comprehension and understanding. Understanding, comprehension, clarity, knowing and confusion arise in being.

# 5

So this is nothing being everything. This is being. All there is is being. And in that being, in that everything, arises separation.

Human beings are the only thing in this appearance that is self-conscious. Self-consciousness is uniquely human. It's the dream. Being arises and dreams it is separate from itself and it then spends a lot of time looking all over the place for that which is everywhere.

So being is all there is, self-consciousness is what arises, and the discovery that there is only being has nothing to do with the seeker. So this – what we're communicating here – has nothing to do with you or me. I haven't got something that you don't have. Being cannot be known.

As a tiny child there is just pure being. Just being. And though a child cries and seems hungry, this is being, this is the expression of being simply crying saying hunger is happening. And then there comes a moment in that child's life when separation happens, when the mother maybe says to the child, "You are

Bill or Mary" and somewhere, energetically, there's a sense of being a separate person. For the first time suddenly there's an energy that contracts into this sense of being separate and there's a feeling in the body that the skin is your limitation, that you live in that boundary, and everything else that's happening is happening outside you.

So life then is happening to you and the moment that separation begins, the moment it begins, seeking begins also, because the sense of separation brings a sense of fear, inadequacy and loss. "I've lost something. What is it? What have I lost? Why have I lost it? Why has this happened to me?" So seeking thereafter happens, and the seeker can only function in seeking. All the time there's separation there can only be seeking for non-separation ... for the need to come home. Until your life is lost you will always wonder why.

We grow up in that world of separation and we meet other people who are living in that world of separation and they all are in agreement that this is a separate world. You are an individual, and you either have to make your life work, or not. That's the basic, simple lesson that is learnt when you're separate. And that whole idea of making your life work, the whole idea of getting things – getting love, getting money, getting power, getting whatever – is actually all a longing to come home. All desire is a reflection of the longing to come home.

Everyone is seeking. And the difficulty is that we grow up and we believe we are individuals and we believe we have an understanding mind, probably, and so we then think that the way we can fill this sense of loss is to try and understand why there's a sense of loss and do something about it, and that's the ignorance. That's the difficulty. The whole difficulty with seeking is that the seeking fuels the separation. Seeking energises separation. So every time we try to find wholeness we're still the separate individual trying to find wholeness. We think that we can get wholeness. We think it's going to happen to us. "I'm going to become enlightened" – or "I could become enlightened. I've heard that I can become enlightened because I've met people in the world who tell me that they are enlightened and that they did A, B and C; they meditated or they self-enquired, or something. So I can get enlightenment." But there is no such thing as an enlightened person. No person in this room will ever become enlightened. The idea of personal enlightenment is the fundamental ignorance that drives people on.

The sense of separation is the whole root of seeking. And even though one's life might work for a while, underneath there's a quiet desperation and there's a drive back to find that oneness. And so we try harder and harder and harder to become enlightened but we will never become enlightened because we're working from a fundamental misconception.

Awakening – what I call awakening – is awakening from a dream, and the dream is to dream of being a separate individual. It's a hypnotic, a very powerful, hypnotic dream. If you walk along Hampstead High Street and ask people they'll tell you, "Yes I am an individual. I have choice and I can do things." That's the dream. And all the time that dream is happening then in a sense you're on a treadmill. You're like a dog chasing its tail. And one of the main difficulties is that the seeker has no idea of what oneness is like, and so is in a continuous state of anticipation.

Awakening is an energetic happening. It's an energetic shift out of contraction into boundlessness. Liberation incidentally brings with it the realisation that all there is is everything. All there is is being. All there is is aliveness. Aliveness is being and all there is in this room right now is aliveness. Things are happening. The door bangs as somebody walks in. Sitting on a chair's happening. Hearing this voice, watching this guy waving his arms around ... that's what's happening. It's life happening. This is being. This is being microphone-ing, this is being chair-ing, this is being being alive.

Anything that you think is happening to you right now is not happening to you, it's simply happening. Life is simply happening.

All there is is being. Nobody can teach you this. This is not a teaching. I can't teach you to sit on a chair. I can't teach you to breathe. I can't teach anybody to be because already there is only being. It's simply a shift out of the perception "I am separate from what is happening" to there only being what is happening. Utterly simple.

When it apparently happens people come and they say, "The constant perfect lover was always here. Life, being. And what is strange is that I can't tell anyone else what this is like because it cannot be known. I can't even tell you Tony what this is."

So, we can talk together and share ideas and to some extent that's the superficial part of this. But energetically there's a sense of something beyond the words. I could describe it maybe as a sense that there is emptiness. It's just emptiness. There's just space sitting there. There's no-one there. There's no-one. There's just space in which things are happening. And the whole idea that you had a life, and you have a life, and you will have a life, simply falls away. The whole idea of karma, cause and effect, action, doing, paths, simply collapses. This message turns everything on its head.

*[Silence]*

○  ○  ○

*And there's nothing you can do. You can just engage with it?*

There's no-one, and so this is beyond engagement.

*Yes, that's exactly right.*

It's no more than sitting on that chair. So when the idea "I haven't got it. I don't see it yet", comes up, that's what is happening. All is being, there is no other.

*Yes, but awakening is beyond cause and effect ...*

Sorry?

*If awakening is beyond cause and effect I think you were saying – beyond cause and effect – no prerequisites ...*

Well, it reveals that cause and effect is a dreamt idea.

*How is it then that seeking can cause it not to happen if you see what I mean? If it's beyond cause and effect, how is it that doing certain things like seeking causes it not to happen?*

But seeking *is* being. It is what's happening. All the time there's apparent seeking there is a belief and expectation of apparent cause and effect. So the whole energy of trying to approach something or seeking to find something is the energy of anticipation in time to get that which is timeless and ungettable. But, let's be clear that I am not saying seek or don't seek. I am describing the apparent dilemma for the "seeker" of always functioning in anticipation. The problem with the seeker is that they think they are something. "I am something. I am something called a human being. And there is something else called 'enlightenment' which I've got to get." It's another something. But awakening is the realisation that what you've been looking for already is nothing and everything. It isn't a something out there. It's everything. This is it. What you're looking for is being this. It was never lost.

Within being arises apparent cause and effect.

*So there's nothing I can do to stop seeking?*

There is no-one, and trying to stop seeking is seeking to stop seeking! It isn't that there's nothing you can do. There's no-one there. All there is is life. All there is is being. It's not happening to anyone. It's just being. The difficulty is that you think you're a person that has to find something. There's nothing to find. There's nothing to wait for. There's absolutely nothing to know or be aware of. This is it.

*So how does recognising that make a difference then?*

Well, give me a ring when it happens. It's just totally beyond description. You don't recognise it, recognising happens. It's stunning. Sorry about that.

*Exactly.*

What is stunning about it is that it isn't ecstasy, it's not bliss. It's totally indescribable. Apparently it happened to somebody in France at a weekend residential. He swam halfway across a river and it happened and there was a guy swimming next to him, and he realised, "There's no way I can tell that guy what this is." It's absolutely stunning, but what's surprising about it is it's totally ordinary and natural. As seekers, there's a veil between the seeker and timeless being. There's a veil of separation. It's an illusory veil but it's very powerful and we can't see through the veil. What we do is to keep on seeing everything "out there". We don't realise that being is not outside or inside, above or below or before or after.

*But does it have a different sort of sensory ...*

No. No. There's no different sense. What I see, you see. Nothing changes but everything is seen as it is.

*The perception is different?*

85

The perception is totally, fundamentally different. However, that perception arises within being.

○ ○ ○

*Tony, in my experience I notice there is something that's aware of all these things; I'm aware of thoughts coming in my head, different kinds of causes, different effects, different feelings, and yet when I'm looking to see "who this me is", there is nothing. And yet, there is something that is aware of what's happening.*

Awareness is once removed. It's still subtly dual. There's awareness of you sitting on a seat. So there are two things. The sitting on a seat and awareness of it. Liberation is totally beyond the watcher, awareness, all of that. Awareness is still an experience. And the difficulty with things like self-enquiry is that people get into this awareness but they can't stay in it, obviously, because it's still in a time-space story. It's still in a dream. It's still transient. It comes and goes. You can't stay in it. And you try to stay in it and you can't.

There's only one constant – being. It never leaves. It doesn't come and it doesn't go away. And we rush round looking for it. "Where is it? Where is it?" You can't do being. Is anybody doing breathing? Is anybody doing sitting on a chair? You can't achieve being. Being is all there is and it speaks through the senses.

The senses are shouting at you "Look, here I am already." Five senses, the feelings and thinking are all beingness simply being, and seekers are looking for that which already is, which is absolutely shouting at the seeker and yet cannot be known.

○  ○  ○

*Where does that place death then, because then there's not being?*

Well, this is about death. You've come here to die. You paid £10 ... *(laughing)* It's quite cheap actually. This is about the dissolution of the dream of the individual. This is about the death of the separate individual.

*Yes, but not real death.*

It is what happens at physical death. At physical death all there is is liberation. Death is the end of the dream of separation of the individual. And it happens either in the body or at the happening we call death.

*But when you say the dream of separation goes, you're still there.*

There is no-one here ... you are talking to nothing.

*The body's here. That's what I mean by real death. Your body is still here.*

This is not anyone's body, it's being bodying.

*But when your body or anybody's physical body goes, well there's nobody there to be liberated or not liberated anyway.*

But that's the whole point which is continually ignored ... there is nobody to be liberated!

*OK, but ...*

No, hold on. You didn't hear that.

*It's not my body. It is body.*

That's body happening.

*But it seems to me to be mine. So whether it seems to be mine, what's the difference?*

The difference is that all the time it seems to be yours, there is a separate entity that dreams that it owns a body. When that dies it'll be suddenly realised that there is only being. That realisation is immeasurable.

*Well, who will realise that?*

No-one.

*Except there won't be anything there.*

No, there will only be nothing and everything, and that is being.

*So why not go on seeking?*

Absolutely. It's great fun. You know, this isn't about seeking or not seeking. What we're talking about here is totally beyond the idea of stopping seeking. Seeking is the absolute divine expression of being. So, there's nothing right or wrong with it. It is aliveness. So nobody gets it right or wrong.

○ ○ ○

*Does dislike still happen for you?*

Oh, disliking and liking still happens for no-one. Everything happens in liberation. But it isn't happening to anyone. It never did of course.

*Has this changed?*

No. There's still disliking apparent people.

*But is your disliking of them the same?*

It is no longer *my* dislike, it is simply dislike.

*Right. But is that different in any way from what it was?*

Everything is totally new. Living in this beingness, everything is totally new. There is no longer a centre that identifies with disliking.

*As in like a memory of previously disliking?*

Memory can still arise and that's another thing that is always new. Everything arises and falls away. Memory, dislike, like, all those things go on apparently happening for no-one. They're just the expression of being. They're happening in free fall.

*But a lot of people who come to hear you talk, think that they've got this "me" and it's not in free fall. It's really fixed. The idea of themselves as being an individual is very fixed.*

Apparently ... until it isn't.

*Until whatever happens.*

Well, separation is totally dreamt.

*Dream's a word I can't get hold of at all because it just sounds like Eastern talk, and I've never understood what dream ...*

OK, so that's fine. Instead you can say it's a belief and an experience that you are a separate individual. You experience that you are separate and that's totally believed and energetically held in place.

*But you can't discover the thing that is the individual?*

You can't because you believe you are separate. You believe you are a separate individual with free will and choice. It's fixed. There's no question about it. For the separate individual, there's no question "I am a separate individual."

*But what you seem to be saying is, after awakening happened then everything still happens but it's not happening to anybody.*

The belief and experience that there is a separate individual is no more.

*So therefore the individual isn't fixed.*

Oh no. It seems fixed all the time individuality is functioning.

*It's the unfixing of a fixation.*

Well, yes. But nobody unfixes it. It just is. Let's say, in simple terms, you go to bed absolutely believing the experiencing that you are an individual. And there's a waking-up the next morning – let's say – and that belief and experience is no longer there.

*OK. I can't make that happen?*

No, because you believe and experience that you are a separate individual. "I am an individual." Why would you want to dissolve? It's your death.

*Oh, because people hear about the problem being you thinking that you're an "I".*

But that's a conceptual idea! Just sharing this in a conceptual way is totally sterile. This isn't about words. This is about something completely beyond words. Words are used. But if you went on just repeating to people "All there is is being. Everything is an expression of being so there's nothing to find. That's it". That would be like saying to an audience of blind people "All there is is seeing. So it's not a problem you know. You can't see but all there is is seeing, so that's OK." What we are describing here is an energetic shift out of apparent separation.

○  ○  ○

*I was just wondering if your relations with people profoundly changed when all this happened to you. Did you lose relationships or gain new ones?*

I don't know. I may have done. But that's not really relevant. There isn't any one. Prior to liberation and after is just what there is. It doesn't get any better or any worse. It's just what it is.

*So nothing majorly changed?*

Not in the sense of values or things getting better for the individual, no. Liberation is not for the individual so this is of no value to the individual. In fact, liberation is the worst thing there is for the individual because it's the end of individuality. So there's nothing to gain and everything to lose. This has lost everything and you still have you.

*After liberation what would make this being get up, eat, go to work etc?*

Before this you believed that you have a motive because you have a life and it is "you" doing every-thing ... making everything happen. "I have my life and I'm going to go and work every day because that will mean I'll get an income and I can pay the bills." After liberation, getting up, working and paying bills happens. Strangely enough it only ever did happen, but you add on "you" to it. You add on the story of you going to work.

*But if there was nobody then nobody would need to go to work; nobody would need to earn money.*

Nothing changes because there is nobody and no need, except in the dream of separation.

*To me it seems then you could just sort of lie down and just be.*

But who is choosing to lie down and be. There is no somebody. Nobody's ever done anything. Nobody will ever do anything. They only believe they're doing it in the dream. Lying down, standing up, eating breakfast, working, is what apparently happens, but you still believe you have to do something to make it happen ... "I am doing it." So being adds on a simulated "me". There is no doer, there is only that which seems to happen.

*If you stop fuelling the fire and just be ...*

But who's going to do that?

*I haven't figured it out.*

That's the difficulty. That's what I'm saying – there isn't anybody that can choose to stop or start fuelling the fire and just be. There isn't anybody that has to do that. Being is just being with or without the dream of the separate entity. You, looking for being, is the expression of being. So being doesn't have any requirements. Whatever is, is unbounded, immaculate wholeness.

○　○　○

*When you look in a mirror, what you see isn't part of being or is it?*

All there is is being.

*But not you actually being?*

There isn't anything that isn't being. The mirror, the eyes, the face, the light, is being. Also the idea of you is being.

*But what's seeing the reflection in the mirror?*

Being is seeing being. So right now being is speaking with being. But the difficulty is that you think you're a person over there and I'm another person and I'm speaking to you and you have to find being. The difficulty is that you think this is something that's happening between two separate objects. The reality is that all of this that's happening is pure being. There is only that.

*It's too simple.*

It's totally and utterly simple and that is how it is hidden from seeking, the one secret the mind cannot unravel. It's so simple it totally confuses the mind. The mind can't possibly see this. There's no way the mind can see this because the mind is locked into time and activity, anticipation and complication. There's no possibility of the mind comprehending this and, more powerfully, it fears its own demise. From the fear of death arises the need to continue which engenders and fosters the promotion of the goal-oriented teachings of becoming.

○  ○  ○

*I can understand there being no person or no choice. What you seem to be saying is there's no past where that person has been conditioned in anything. Is that correct? There is no past?*

There appears to be a past and the conditioning that arises. There is only timeless being appearing as that.

*So in that sense this didn't happen. So when is the present?*

There isn't any.

*There is no present either?*

This is no thing happening. There's no past, there's no future, there's no above, there's no below, there's no inner, there's no outer. There is no present moment. Show me the present moment ... where can it be?

*Is that because those are concepts?*

Yes. They're only the dream or the belief and experience of a separate person arising in this time, goals, meaning, purpose, cause and effect, karma, past lives ... all that dream story arises as this. The moment we become separate we hope for an answer so we attach to that hope the idea "Oh there must be a meaning. Why is this happening? Why aren't I in paradise? Where is goodness? Why have I lost it? There must be a meaning for this life I have, so what I must do is find meaning." So we go to people who teach us meaning. We go to enlightenment masters who tell us, "Yes there is a meaning. I'll teach you how to find meaning through effort, sacrifice, dedication, devotion, change, personal refinement of the body-mind or whatever other teaching of becoming."

*If there's no meaning, what stops you from being a couch potato?*

Nothing. If couch potatoing happens it happens. There's nobody who can choose to be a couch potato or not be one. So a lot of people – teachers – say "Well Tony Parsons is teaching spiritual laziness." Of course, they're not really hearing what's being said. They think that Tony Parsons is saying, "There's nothing you can do so go and watch *East Enders"*, but actually that isn't the message.

The fundamental message is, there is no such thing as a separate entity with free will or choice and so nobody can choose to watch *East Enders* or not watch it. What is apparently done or not done is completely irrelevant to being.

*So when you're attached to your identity you try to bend things, to want things and do things.*

You dream that you are doing those things and need to do them in order to get more things.

*So that just disappears?*

What disappears is the one who feels separate. There's only being. It can't be conceived of. It can't be described. It cannot even be known.

*This story is so compelling. This is so compelling.*

It's compelling and fascinating to you. If you take "you" out of the happening it's just what's happening. What's compelling about what's happening right now? I mean it's just happening. What's the compulsion?

*It's a thought story that feels very real.*

But where is that story right now? What's happening in that story?

*What's happening in that story?*

Where's this going right now? Is there a story? What's happening there? What is sensed there right now in the body?

*Tiredness.*

So that's what there is. That is this, beingness. But the mind gets hold of the tiredness and says "Well, that is your tiredness and so what you need to do now is get to bed, or not work so hard, or use your energy in a better way." And there you are back in a story trying to make things better for you.

*Yes. And it's because the tiredness is there.*

No. It's really because you are still there taking ownership of the tiredness. Then when you're in bed and you've slept for 12 hours you'll take ownership of feeling better. It's always telling you "You're going to feel better – or worse." It's the greatest and most powerful addiction there is … you.

○  ○  ○

*Can I change the subject?*

Yes.

*How do you know if this is the last life you're going to live?*

It isn't the last or first life. It's no-one's life at all. This isn't your life. There isn't anyone who has their own life, there is only life.

*To you then, past lives are irrelevant?*

Well, obviously, because there's no-one.

*Yes, OK.*

There's no past because there's no-one. The mind wants things to continue so it creates the idea that you've had a past life. Usually as a great healer or a queen or something! It's never a lavatory cleaner! *(laughing)* And then you will die and become another great queen – or a lavatory cleaner. *(laughing)*

It's the individual in the dream wanting always to continue, it's called self-survival, that's why it goes on seeking because it wants things to continue. It doesn't want to come to an end. It doesn't want to die. The last thing it wants is liberation. The last thing it wants is absence, and absence is liberation. But most seekers want something. They want to be enlightened and they don't think that's the end of them. They think that they will become enlightened and they think other people are enlightened.

○   ○   ○

*Can you say something about no past, no future, because memory seems to have failed at that? If it was seen, if it was known that there was no past and there is no future, that would be tantamount to awakening wouldn't it, in a sense?*

No, awakening is absence. It's nothing. The end of separation is awakening. When there's an awakening from the dream of being separate there is only being. But in that being can arise an apparent memory about something that happened last week. But the memory is being this. If you look at memory it only arises in this. Memory arises *(claps)*. It's another aliveness. Remembering something is aliveness. It doesn't then mean that there was a last week.

*No, no, but the sense of being trapped in time, place and person seems to be real.*

Oh well, everything in the dream totally convinces the dreamer that that is the reality. Everything in the dream convinces the dreamer that they are an individual in a world that is in time, and that life is happening to them and it has a meaning and a purpose.

*But there's absolutely no antidote to that?*

Except the dissolution of the dreamer. There's no antidote for dreaming except waking up.

*Yes, but there's no remedy for that at all is there?*

Well there doesn't need to be because there's nothing wrong with that.

*Nothing wrong with what?*

Dreaming. Separation. It is the expression of being. In separation there is a feeling of disquiet and then for the seeker that creates a sense of loss and a sense of suffering which then impels them to try and either escape from that suffering or to resolve it. The difficulty for the seeker is that they can neither escape from it or resolve it because that very effort fuels the sense of separation.

*That just happens in being too doesn't it?*

Well, there is only being. It doesn't just happen in being and not in being. There is only being and seeking arises in being.

*So there is no remedy because you can't stop yourself?*

But there doesn't need to be because there's nothing wrong with suffering and loss and seeking. It's just what it is.

*So the clarity to understand this stuff is of no aid whatsoever?*

No.

*I mean there's absolutely no point in coming to listen to this?*

No, none at all.

*But truly there isn't?*

No, but are you going to stop coming?

*I can't stop coming.*

Because there is no-one to choose either way. No amount of concepts, no amount of words or ideas are ever going to open anybody's eyes. They're just words.

○ ○ ○

*Tony, you spoke about an energetic shift and I am imagining that there could be some kind of transmitting of an energy that would allow this apparent body-mind over here to ...*

No, absolutely not, because there's no-one that has anything. There's no-one that has anything therefore there's no-one to give anything to anyone else. And because there is no-one else there's no-one to give it to anyway. The whole idea of transmission of energy or enlightenment from one to another is based on the misconception of personal enlightenment or the idea that there is *something* separate called "enlightenment" that can somehow be possessed and then passed on or given to someone else, like so much candy.

*What is the energetic thing?*

Being is boundlessness. There is only boundless-ness. There is only being and there isn't anything else but that. Try and find something that isn't being. There is only being and what's amazing about it is that in that being arises the idea that there isn't being ... that there is a me looking for being, looking for enlightenment. This is absolute immaculate wholeness and in that immaculate wholeness arises the idea that this isn't immaculate wholeness.

But it's not only an idea. It's energetically held. The seeker is energetically holding on to "me" – "I'm in this body and separate from what's out there!" The holding on to "me" is an energetic contraction out of fear and the need to survive. That apparent contraction can dissipate into boundlessness. The energetic shift *apparently* happens out of the absence of separation and therefore doesn't happen to anyone.

○  ○  ○

*Some time ago you said nothing's happening.*

Yes, absolutely.

*So how can everything be happening and nothing's happening?*

That's the mystery. This *(claps hands)* is nothing happening. It's nothing. It's no-thing clapping its hands. The difficulty for the seeker is that it thinks that that is *something* that's real, it's happening in time to the seeker. Because the seeker thinks they are something they can only see everything else as a lot of other somethings. They daren't see the no-thing ... it is too frightening.

*What's the answer to that?*

It's a mystery. There is no answer. But it doesn't matter about seeing that or not seeing that. This is it. Already this is the play of being. Even the frustration "I'm not seeing this" is the absolute play of being.

*So it's not cause and effect; it's nothing to do with proper conditions?*

There aren't any conditions or cause and effect, except in the dream of becoming.

*But if you bang your hand on a wall or something ...*

It hurts.

*The effect is that it hurts.*

It certainly seems to.

*So why is that not cause and effect?*

It only appears to be cause and effect. In the manifestation there seems to be cause and effect, and the difficulty for the dreamer is that they then apply some sort of fixed reality and meaning to that. And therefore they then follow that by saying, "Well if I meditate I will become still. That's cause and effect. Then I will reach the goal." There is no I and there is no goal and no time to reach it.

*So there's apparent cause and effect, not actual cause and effect?*

There isn't anything that's actual. All manifestation is both real and unreal. It is simply being. Cats are being. Trees are being. Walls are being. Human beings are being and dream that they are separate from being.

*So therefore nothing lies outside of the dream?*

Oh yes, the dream is the dream of self-consciousness. The dream, or, if you prefer, the belief and experience of being separate, is uniquely human. No cat feels separate. Trees don't feel separate. Have you ever come across a self-conscious tree? We walk round as being looking for being, that's the dream from which there can be an awakening ... apparently.

*But if there were no humans there'd still be trees and cats?*

No.

*No? There wouldn't? It's like the old saying, if a tree falls in the forest, but you have no-one there to hear ...*

Yes. Or if a man's standing in the desert and there's no woman for 2,000 miles, is he still wrong?

*(Laughter)*

○   ○   ○

*I've read that when you become enlightened or free there will be peace and joy and bliss.*

It's a way to sell something. You know the whole enlightenment teaching is about "you" getting something and the irony is that enlightenment is about loss. It is about there being no "you". There are a lot of teachers who will give this idea lip service. They will start by saying "There is only oneness. Nobody can do anything about enlightenment. It's totally beyond anything – but in the meantime what you need to do in order to find that out is to meditate or self-enquire." ... or whatever is the agenda. You have to prepare yourself to discover that there's no-one and nothing to prepare for. *(laughing)*

*What's your take on all these different descriptions like awakening, self-realisation, liberation?*

Well, I use the words "awakening" and "liberation" because I can't think of anything else to use. But there is no such thing as awakening or liberation because nothing's happening anyway. There is only the play of being, so nothing needs to be liberated. But for the seeker those are just words. Those purely conceptual teachings don't illuminate the apparent dilemma of the seeker and they also totally ignore the most powerful thing of all, and that is the energetic element.

Awakening is an energetic shift. It's about the aliveness of this ... what is happening. There is a gift within the essence of what is sensed. You can go on repeating conceptual ideas forever but ideas are stories about this. For me awakening is the nearest description I can get to what I see as the apparent awakening from the dream or belief and experience that there is a separate individual. However, there is no-one that awakens.

*So people are going to go "pop" around you are they?*

No, absolutely not, because this has nothing to do with being around me because there is no "me". But what the seeker is meeting and communicating with is no-thing, and when the apparent something meets nothing there can be an energy shift. Also in that freedom there is no longer any demand or expectation laid on anyone and the whole sense of struggle and effort can fall away. Everyone is already seen in wholeness. This is all about rediscovering something that is already being. But by its very nature, it isn't anybody's to give or receive.

*So I'm the dreamer rather than the dream character, or a bit of both?*

The dreaming is only about separation. After the dream, after apparent liberation, there are still characteristics. There's still a body-mind that has characteristics ... that is aliveness apparently happening.

*As a dreamed character then?*

No, the dream is only about the dream of being a separate entity.

*But the dream's over?*

Yes, in apparent liberation the dream of being separate is no more.

*The curiosity is that adults perpetuate the illusion of separation but there's no way of stopping the illusion because the minute you name your child you've given them an identity.*

There's nothing wrong with that. That's being playing a game of identification. And everything in the world reinforces that. Labelling, naming, everything you are taught in order to deal with the world. So you grow up trying to make your life work. And one of the ways you make your life work is to try to know everything. "I've got to know everything so that I can control it." Maybe when you're 18 years old, you fall in love with this absolutely divine woman. You fall in love and suddenly there is the unknown again because falling in love is a very, very similar taste to this. And you fall totally in love with this absolutely divine being ... for at least a week. *(laughing)*

*And then what happens?*

And then you try to know her. And then the clock's ticking again and you're back into knowing something so that you can control it. Or you dream that you are.

So we try to build a world apparently that we think we know. We think we're doing this. It's being doing it. We believe we go on doing it and so the world becomes known and dull ... and seemingly safe. This communication is about totally reawakening to the absolute wonder and naked, vibrant innocence of childlikeness. It's incredibly freeing but it's also dangerous. It is being in unknowing.

*Is there fear?*

Oh fear can still arise. Anything arises ... for no-one ... It's absolute, boundless, passionate aliveness.

*You know it sounds so fantastic.*

Yes, but it's fantastic for no-one.

*Does the passionate aliveness continue?*

It doesn't continue because it never started or stopped, it never comes or goes. It's eternal.

You're seeing everything through a veil. You're seeing everything from the perception of a separate dreamer in a time story. From something seeing something else only. So you don't see the wall for what it is. You see it for what you dream it as ... and you dream it as a separate something ... not as nothing being everything.

*Right. Not only am I a dream seeker, everything I see is a dream?*

It appears to be.

*Right, and then if awakening happens there's something else.*

In a sense this is to do with nothing and everything. Or let's call it nothing and something just for the sake of this conversation. The dream seeker only experiences themselves as something and also therefore sees the wall as something else. When there is no dream the wall is seen as nothing and something. What the dream seeker can't see, and is frightened to see, is the nothingness in everything that manifests.

*And so if there's no-one, then ...*

Then everything is being nothing and something.

*Right. So then they're the same thing.*

Yes, but in a sense everything is perceived differently because it's seen as it really is, which is nothing arising as everything, which is beingness.

*But we already ... there has never not been no-one?*

Oh, no. Absolutely. There is only beingness. But

now we're back into parables I'm afraid. There is only nothing appearing as everything and in the everything arises the idea that there is an individual who only sees something separate.

*I get really tangible, deep feelings of what you're talking about.*

Yes. This is all about sensing the immediate vibrant aliveness in the senses that are this gift of unknowing.

○ ○ ○

*What's your sense of standing here right now? Is there any way of describing that?*

Warmth. There's being warmth, excitement, feet on the ground. Somebody's moved just over there. Cars going by.

*But they don't add up to a kind of something?*

No, they just are what's apparently happening. The formless in form … beingness.

*OK so they're not being joined. I think maybe we're joining them.*

Oh, the separate entity joins them and makes them into a story that can be known. And they also dream that what is happening is happening to them and it has meaning about getting somewhere.

*OK, what I experience – it's absolutely true – is an incredible feeling of vulnerability as though the shell's come off.*

Yes.

*And I kind of get a bit like I've got goosebumps. I just feel really like ...*

Risky?

*Yes. It feels like something has been peeled off. Something like a prawn or something. If you peel off the casing there's just no protection. And it feels uncomfortable. If I don't go into a story it just feels uncomfortable physically.*

The way you get back to being you and feeling safe is to go into the apparent story of you in time.

*Yes, but do you just cope with that vulnerability and go with it?*

No, there is no-one to cope with anything, there is just nakedness.

*It just all happens then?*

It's like being naked and open to everything and there's a sense of risk about it. Everything is suddenly unknown and very alive ... there are no filters.

*You get used to it?*

There is no-one to get used to anything. There are no artificial filters that you previously provided as an individual. That's why it's got nothing to do with what people call detachment. It's totally full-on aliveness ... for no-one.

*Tony, this sense of vulnerability is because all the filters have come off. I sometimes wonder what that was? What was that sense of security, those filters?*

It's a false sense that first of all there is someone. "I am a separate person and everything out there is separate from me and in some way or other is threatening. So I put up filters. I protect myself by trying to inhibit feelings. Another way I protect myself from those things that arise as threatening is to get to understand what they are." Basically we try to understand what there is out there that seems threatening so that we can know it and control it. It's an artificial filter that we seem to construct in the hypnotic dream of being separate.

*I remember once this vulnerability and saying to myself "This is this and that's that," and feeling immediately much more secure.*

Quite often people say to me that openness has happened. "The other night this happened." And immediately the mind came back with a story or anything to get them back to being a person. "Oh god, let me think of something ... my bank overdraft for instance, anything that will bring me back into being an individual." And people apparently have games that go on keeping them stuck in individuality for fear of boundlessness.

*So in a sense are you saying instead of being a reference point on a map, you become the whole map?*

Yes, I like that. But there is no you to be anywhere.

*The sense of location is something that's definitely going on?*

In liberation there can still be a sense of location where there is just what's going on. There are no reference points. There's nothing that's going on for something. There's just what's going on.

*And there's no difference between being anywhere and anywhere else?*

No of course not. There is only beingness.

# 6

*When I get back to the U.S. my parents are going to be picking me up at the airport, and I was trying to think of how to describe this week (laughing), and so I thought I will say, "Well I went to England to learn something from a man who says he is not there, who has nothing to teach, and I am not there either. It is all pointless and it is hopeless and I paid good money for it, and I am thinking of going back in November next year." (laughing) I think that needs some work, you know.*

Yes, I think so, they could take you directly to an institution.

*I have learned by experience, with the Tony Parsons happening, that when you go home the best thing to do is to find yourself a quiet corner and not say anything to anybody, because you cannot explain the unexplainable. It's really best just to say as little as possible.*

o  o  o

The only thing about all of this is that it's very easy

to get back into the concepts about this, about "me-ing" and "be-ing" and about there being no-one, there only being oneness, and all of those ideas, and really lose the main essence of this message.

You described telling somebody when you go home, "I met this man who says there is no-one there, and I am not there and there is no meaning." All of that is the part of this message that leaves the apparent seeker with nothing to get hold of. However, the most vital and relevant communication in the open secret is the vibrant aliveness of just what is happening ... seeing, hearing, breathing and thinking and also the arising of feelings.

We tend to have feelings that arise and then we poke them with a stick. *(laughing)* The mind will say, "Well, why do I feel anger or sadness?" So we must work out why, or we must do something with anger or sadness like honour it, or share it with other people. We can't just let it be there! And this message is absolutely about this aliveness, the aliveness that is simple and present and is the only constant.

This is the song of love. The song of freedom is in our bodies, in our senses, all the time constantly being and speaking to us through the body. And the whole thing about not being here, and there being no meaning, is just incidental to that absolute passionate aliveness.

o  o  o

*So is the aliveness as real as the nothing?*

The aliveness is nothing being something, so the aliveness is both real and unreal; nothing appearing as being alive.

This is nothing *(claps hands)* clapping. We tend to think in terms of being in a place called "liberation" or whatever you like, or even being in a place called "being". Being is in this, *(claps hands)*, all is being. It's as simple and immediate as that. What is happening is this, aliveness, being. It can't be known and doesn't need to be known and held onto.

*I once read a book years ago by a healer and he said that it's nearer, closer than breathing, nearer than hands and feet, so it's kind of right here.*

It's not even close. It's not "right here" it's all there is, and is not. What we look for is constantly already in what is, aliveness, what is happening. It is constantly all there is ... and isn't.

*I don't know if anyone else has experienced this. A couple of times I have just been doing something very ordinary like drying my hands and I've suddenly looked down as if I am seeing my hands for the first time. It was so different from all the other times that I've apparently seen them, but I just couldn't let go, I just wanted to, well I did, I sort of just left them there until it just eventually went.*

Yes, it's amazing, it is the immediacy of this, that is where it is, the secret is in the essence of aliveness.

*We totally overlook it, don't we, we don't even see it any more?*

Oh, we don't notice this at all, we are always looking

for what's next. We are always looking out there, when it is actually right with us right in this. We are sitting on it.

But, the amazing paradox is that the seeker's distraction is also immaculate being.

*Your example is perfect when you clap your hands, because that is exactly what it is. It's just a clapping, just a moment of amazement, wow, it is just like, wow. It is so ordinary, it's so completely ordinary, but it's so beautiful.*

Well, as my wife says, it is a sudden wow that becomes a gentle, subtle, constant wow.

o  o  o

*What is the mechanism that makes separation possible?*

Well there isn't a mechanism, it's just what is apparently happening. What happens is being separate and there is a sort of fascination about, "I am separate and I can do it. I can do this." It's a fascinating dream.

*Is it just the fascination and you get caught in the fascination?*

Yes, but it doesn't matter because it's perfect. It's not wrong, it is absolutely the perfect game that being plays of being totally fascinated with being a separate entity and doing it all. The world that we see is an absolute expression of what appears to be individual creativity or action. So it is being arising as totally fascinated by the idea of being separate and doing things.

*Tony, what is the difference between having a glimpse, or glimpses, and an awakening?*

There isn't any. What we call a glimpse, which we think is half a second, is actually eternity, so that is awakening. It is the being of oneness for nobody.

*Because I have had glimpses, yet I don't feel that awakening has happened.*

Well, it has.

*Don't tell my wife.*

I won't tell your wife. *(laughing)* The sweetest thing I ever heard was from an American, who said "The worst nightmare is that my wife becomes enlightened before I do." *(laughter)* And it doesn't necessarily mean that anything else will happen.

*Well, life goes on. But liberation is not there.*

Well it is, it is all there is except you don't think it is.

*Yes, OK.*

I could send you a certificate if you like? *(laughter)*

*Do you charge for them?*

Grade three awakening. *(laughter)*

*Like a report card?*

Quite expensive though. *(laughter)*

○  ○  ○

*Tony, there must be a centre of perception for you?*

Perception arises in being but without a centre or a perceiver.

*I don't understand.*

There is no perceiver to perceive something else ... there is only what is, isness, being. Perception arises in being but being can't be perceived or known.

*OK.*

It is being. There is only being. Coming from a practical point of view, this body-mind organism will perceive the door opening and walk through it. It does walk through walls but only on Thursdays! *(laughter)*

In other words, everything just goes on as it did before, but there is only being.

*So even though there is the sense of sight, that's not perception?*

It is *nobody's* perception ... it is just perception happening, but it is happening within being. So the functions still apparently happen but there isn't a centre *from which* they happen.

*Sure, but life is experienced also, presumably through senses?*

That happens, but for no-one and all within being. It is timeless.

*And there is more of an awareness of that rather than a focus?*

There isn't an awareness or a focus at all, there is only being.

*OK, so that's not separate from the appearance of objects, at all?*

No, not at all. That is all and everything …

*So it is "one with"?*

No, it is absolutely not at one with it, it is no-thing being everything. And it is a mystery because the mystery is that we always think that it should be known in some way or another, or perceived.

As I have said before, the Buddhists' idea of ultimate enlightenment is the knowing of the known. But, there needs to be a known and a knower so this is still locked into the story of two, just as awareness or mindfulness is.

All there is is being … it cannot be known … it is the mystery and wonder of unknowing … indefinable, ineffable isness. It's not some amazing place to be in, somewhere else, it is what's in this room right now, that's all there is to it. Totally, absolutely, naturally, ordinarily this.

*And even though there is no caring about this at all, isn't it possible that further aspects of the mystery could at some point be revealed?*

Why do we always want more! This utter madness and insatiable greed that wants more than everything. It's amazing. I can't imagine that there could be any more than nothing and everything. *(laughter)*

*But you used the word "mystery" you see.*

But for me the mystery is the unknowing, the wonderfully risky aliveness in free fall. The mind can't ever see how there could just be being, that there could be something that is there that isn't known, because the mind wants to know, wants to be in control. So what I am saying is that for the mind it's an absolute mystery. For liberation there is no mystery, there is just what there is, but it is apparently arising in unknowing.

*So are you saying, when you say "mystery", you mean that it's unexplainable?*

It is unexplainable to the mind, essentially, whereas in liberation there is no longer anything that needs an explanation ... that needs knowing.

*It's because we want to narrow the thinking, we can't squeeze it into thought.*

No, you can't possibly. You can't know it. It's like the eye trying to see itself.

○　○　○

*And, the enduring paradox is that as long as there is separation there is a seeker, and as long as there is a seeker there is a separation. It's a paradox. The beginning of the end of that paradox, is in seeing that separation is that?*

There isn't a beginning. You could say the awakening, the timeless wonder of this, reveals that there was apparently separation. But the recognition of being separate is only the recognition of separation. It's another experience. There is certainly something that is enlightening about that, but it isn't any more than that. In other words, you then have someone who is enlightened about understanding and comprehending that the seeking is fuelling the separation.

But really I think you are just talking about clarity. What blows everything apart is nothing. You are walking along the road and then there is nothing. Bang! And then after that nothing is ever quite the same. It wouldn't matter if you went on for the rest of your life without anything more happening, still everything is different thereafter. It is never the same, you will never go back to where you were just before.

*So Tony, is it the experience of being nowhere or everywhere or both?*

It is indescribable.

*So nowhere and everywhere are the same thing?*

Yes, there is already only nothing being everything, the absolute being relative.

○   ○   ○

*Tony, I feel this, not just here, but when I am reading, I feel this sort of splitting being, where on the one hand there are these words and concepts like "being" and then on the other hand there is the, I suppose you could call it, poetic expressions like "beloved", "Home, with a capital H"; I can't connect them, they seem to be opposites, like male and female, or something like that.*

Well words are always in battle, they are dualistic ... based on subject-object. It is possible to analyse everything that is said and expose the futility of verbal expression on this subject ... but it is a shallow activity born of the frustration of not being able to sense where the words are pointing.

*But it's more, it is not just words, it's not just about words, it is actually about the kind of taste of it all. In a way I think you are saying that I am caught up in the descriptions ... I suppose sometimes that's all I've got.*

No, that's alright, I mean there is obviously nothing wrong with being locked into a place. And there are definitely, with all of this, words, concepts and ideas, and even the recognition that seeking fuels separation is still another concept. It's like going down the road and there is a sign to the left saying "Let's talk about being", and there is a sign to the right that says "Being", so what we are doing here, most of the time, is talking about being. And that is OK, that is what is apparently happening. However, what's also happening here is that the questions dry up ... the seeking mind gives up because it can't get an answer that would fuel another question.

*That's what's happening, up to now.*

Yes, maybe. The seeker will find any way not to be, because the seeker is scared of being, because it would mean that the seeker would then cease to be, to exist.

*I think I know that. It does seem though that during these days I have found that I don't try to manipulate experience.*

In a sense, there is only this energy but it just so happens here that what we are doing is talking about being.

*But energetically this is quite different for me. Compared to any other group that I have ever come across, this is the most energetic for me.*

○  ○  ○

*Tony, when you say there is no cause and effect ... I mean, for instance, you wrote* The Open Secret *and the fact is that people come to meetings and something happens. I hear you say that there is no cause and effect. Is that because there can be no relationship between dream and reality?*

But I didn't write that book and we are not having a meeting and there is no-one here. It only appears that I wrote a book and then people heard about this and came. That is an appearance, and then the mind thinks that proves that there is such a thing as cause and effect. This goes back to this strange paradox that actually there is nothing happening.

*So it's like there is cause and effect, but you just can't go there?*

There only appears to be cause and effect, meaning the story.

*There appears to be, but one can't go there?*

The appearance of cause and effect is no more than the appearance of this cup. It appears to be a cup, and there appears to be something called "cause and effect".

*But as soon as you enter it ...*

It is what appears to be happening. It arises in being, as everything else does. It only arises in being, and it is both real and unreal.

*I don't think it is understandable.*

No, it doesn't matter anyway, but being can't be understood or known.

*But if you were demonstrating the laws of cause and effect, and you were showing simply how cause and effect works, and you were holding that cup and you let go and it smashed on the ground, would that be a demonstration of how cause and effect didn't operate?*

It would demonstrate how cause and effect appear to operate. But the fundamental realisation arises out of liberation that cause and effect is totally and utterly meaningless. It is only the mind that thinks in terms of story. But there isn't anywhere to go. There is nowhere that anything has ever been.

*Tony, that paradox, all that can be said about it is that it's there but it's not there?*

Yes, it's a description of something that is just not comprehensible. Suddenly it is. People phone me and say, "I have been listening to you talk all of this gobbledygook for a year, you know, there is no cause and effect, and suddenly it is all totally clear." It has now been seen that that's how it is, but before that it has to just be a concept.

*It is so difficult for the mind to get around.*

It is impossible.

# 7

All there is is this. And this is being. Being ... being room, being bodies, being seats. All there is is being. So tonight we're going to share together a rare and revolutionary message.

We can look together at the nature of the open secret. It's a secret all the time there's anyone looking for it. It's open because it's all there is.

All there is is being and being is both nothing and everything. There is no other.

In all there is arises the idea of separation. This is being appearing as a separate entity and dreaming that it is a separate individual. So what appears is the dreamer, and the dreamer's function is only to dream in separation as an individual. And when that takes place, there's a feeling of discomfort, there's a feeling of loss. So from the moment of separation as a tiny child there is seeking. The clock starts ticking and seeking happens. And that seeking is the longing to fill that sense of loss.

All teachings of becoming teach you that you are a separate individual and you have a choice and you have to make an effort to get to somewhere. And that whole belief system reinforces the power of the dream and the sense of separation. It's just the dream. It's a story. It's the apparent story of being seeking being.

But it is possible, when there's a readiness, and it's nobody's readiness, that something else will be heard ... another possibility that's totally revolutionary will be heard. And what can be heard is that there is an awakening from the dream. But it won't be the dreamer that awakens from the dream. The dreamer, the seeker, suddenly is no more and that is the awakening.

It's a fundamental shift in perception that happens. But there is no-one who can make that happen nor will the awakening happen to anyone. No-one can do it for you and you can't do it because you, the seeker, can only function in the moving story of finding, of anticipating. "It's going to be the next time. It's going to be after the next meditation. It's going to be on the next page ... the answers could be on the next page." The dreamer always lives in anticipation. The clock is always ticking.

Liberation incidentally brings with it the realisation that there is no clock, there is no dreamer, there is no seeker, no guru, there is no awakening or liberation ... all there is is being.

So, together perhaps we will find that questions can arise and, in a sense, there won't be any answers because there is no answer. The answer to life is that there is no answer. Life is the answer. So the mind will probably go on fighting and trying to find something that it can do and choose, but here it may be discovered that that's not possible. There is an argument that questioning keeps on regenerating itself through dialogues, but that need not happen here. The mind discovers here that there is nowhere to get to and so it can give up.

So life, this, is apparently happening. It's simply happening in nothing. This is a totally fundamental shift that's so simple it completely confounds the mind. It's just aliveness with no-one being alive.

○   ○   ○

*Tony, at the moment there seems to be a sort of slight background dull sense of dissatisfaction, or something being missing in the mind-body ... and that is totally OK.*

Is it? *(laughter)* Why does it have to be totally OK?

*Well, I don't feel like I am trying to get out of that, I am just wanting to talk about it.*

So you have now started telling a story; that there is dissatisfaction and that it is totally OK. So presumably it is totally OK with *someone* that there is dissatisfaction; that's a story.

*So, it is a comment, a comment on experience really.*

You are back into a story about it, things being OK. What this is saying is that all there is is what there is, including dissatisfaction. But let's hold on to that

... there is dissatisfaction and then there might be the idea that that's absolutely OK. In that sense they are both what there is, but the difficulty is that the mind then links up the idea that that is totally OK with it. And this is the beginning of the whole process of story about an individual getting somewhere called "being OK".

*There is some sense of dissatisfaction, loss or whatever and there is some sense of that being OK as well, and also there is something about that being OK to have that.*

Yes, go on.

*There is an idea which is that seeing dissatisfaction as OK or being aware of it is in some way useful.*

But there is something going on in there about dealing with whatever arises. In other words, whatever arises, if it is seen in a certain way as being OK, or is seen in awareness, then somewhere that deals with it.

*Right.*

And so you have still got a businessman in there. However sophisticated that may be, there is still something dealing with what is happening, or trying to.

*Which is also a meditative-type angle isn't it? When we see that, it's different.*

There is nothing to be done about that, that's what it is.

*That feeling of disquiet, where does it come from?*

Nothing. *(laughter)*

*It doesn't denote anything?*

There you go! *(laughter)* Actually, "Does it denote anything?", is the same thing as "awareness of it", or the feeling that "It's OK, we will deal with it. Does it denote anything? I have to work it out, analyse it, and then I can deal with it." There can't just be dissatisfaction!

*There is definitely something of anxiety and fear here.*

All of that is what's happening. It's just what's happening; fear, adrenaline, cup of tea, adrenaline settling down again, cigarette ...

*It feels like a remedy has to be found.*

Directly the mind is involved, then remedies and analysis and answers to the way to deal with it arise. "How can I deal with this?" Fear arises – actually in timelessness – but then the mind gets hold of it and the clock starts ticking and now we've got to do something with it. A story begins; it's another story. There are billions of little stories going on about how to deal with what's happening; there is no possibility of just letting it be what it is. And in the end the dreamer is seeking a better situation, usually, or if it's pure pleasure there is also something behind it saying, "How can we hold on to this?" Because somewhere it is known that the pleasure won't last. "Oh, can this be permanent?" or "It's here, isn't it wonderful, but I know somehow it's going to go soon." In separation there is a continuously meddling function. Until your life is lost you will always be meddling with it.

*It always spoiled my massages, (laughter) because a couple of minutes into it and it's like, "This is going to end." (laughter)*

○ ○ ○

*So, Tony, when the mind gets hold of these things, can you explain the difference between the functioning mind and the mind that's interfering? Because things arise and you might have a thought about the future and there might be some anxiety ... is that ...?*

Dream-thinking.

*Is that dream-thinking?*

Yes.

*So you are saying that in liberation things just happen and there is no need to consider any of them?*

In liberation, dream-thinking happens but it is very much diminished. It still happens and it is just another appearance happening to no-one, in free fall. There is no-one taking delivery of it.

*But you would distinguish between dream-thinking and functional thinking?*

There is no need to distinguish because both apparent happenings are beingness and so one is no more significant or valuable than the other. There is nothing calculating any more – that is that and this is this – it is just what it is. But in order to answer the question I'm describing it.

*But what bit would actually hear all there is is this?*

There isn't anything that is hearing, all there is is this. There is no reporting of it. It can't be known! In answering the question I am telling you what it is like; this is a description of that which is being. Dream-thinking is simply being dream-thinking. But in describing it obviously there are words you use, but in reality there is nothing reporting, because there is nothing perceiving. In other words, there is no longer a judge in there trying to work out the value, or otherwise, of a particular thought.

*There is a tendency to think that something needs to be heard and someone needs to hear that.*

Well, when there is, when somebody asks a question of nothing, nothing seems to respond and in describing the apparent situation moves back into addressing the question from the point of view of the questioner. It destroys what is behind the question but it also uses language to attempt to describe that which can't be described. Language is necessarily dualistic.

*You don't have to mull questions over?*

No, of course not. I was just describing to somebody outside that this is so utterly spontaneous because there is nothing in there, because what is being said here basically doesn't come out of the mind; the mind isn't in this at all. This is just coming out of nothing, so there is no monitoring of it. And there is nothing in the way of what's being said. If the response was from the mind's understanding you would be getting totally different answers that would be locked into logic, story and the idea of becoming.

o  o  o

*Seems like what is going on here is very dangerous in a way because you are ruining the dream ...*

Yes. But it is only dangerous for the illusory individual locked in separation. There is no-one ruining an apparent dream. The ignorance of the dream of becoming is exposed.

*And we can't go back?*

There is no forward or back. Compassion is the destroyer of illusion, it isn't helping ladies over the road or helping people get through life. Compassion doesn't help the separate individual, it exposes the dream of separation and leaves freedom. Unconditional love doesn't recognise that there is a separate person who needs help ... that is the freeing nature of the boundlessness that is palpable when we are together.

o  o  o

*Tony, would you say that the self-consciousness and the seeker are the same thing?*

Yes, self-consciousness is separation, "I am a separate entity."

*So would you say also that, in some bodies if you like, there is more self-consciousness than others?*

It would appear to be like that, yes.

*So there can therefore be a diminishing of self-consciousness?*

There can be, but that has no relevance to awakening. Being isn't the slightest bit interested in degrees of its own apparent self-consciousness. All and everything is the expression of being. The apparent individual can be as neurotic, as quiet and still, as intelligent, as schizophrenic or self-conscious as you like, and this is all the play of being. It is already immaculately whole.

*In the story, would you say that there is a correlation between awakening and people who are perhaps more at ease generally ...*

With themselves?

*With themselves, yes. The correlation between that state and awakening.*

No, no absolutely not, there is no correlation. But obviously, in the story, there are apparent people who are easier with being separate than others. What that "someone" is like has absolutely nothing to do with the reality that there isn't someone. There doesn't have to be less someone for there to be no someone. *(laughing)*

*Well, people do talk about neurosis falling away.*

Yes, it is very tempting and somehow logical to believe that if you could quiet your agitation, enlightenment might be more available. That is a confused personal belief.

*Surely in a sense someone who isn't so self-conscious wouldn't be interested in liberation?*

There aren't any rules. And anyway it doesn't matter how interested anybody is in so-called liberation; already there is wholeness. Being interested or even passionately devoted to finding enlightenment is what is apparently happening in the fairy story of seeking what already is.

○　○　○

*We are going to climb a mountain this afternoon, and I realised I was thinking that would be great, because I feel I want to be away from voices and stuff. And that's just mind, it's got nothing to do with ...*

Yes, it wouldn't matter if you climbed 60 mountains this afternoon, it's no different than this, it is just that you think it is. Wherever you apparently go there is only ever silence, being. So-called voices and stuff are simply being, just as your apparent need to escape from them is.

*It's a judgment about what's it all about?*

Yes, because all this speaking that is going on here is all simply silence sounding. That's why I would never try to impose the idea of a silent retreat because that idea is based on the misconception that not speaking is silence and silence is somehow "better" than apparent sound. However, in these meetings much "silence" happens organically because the mind just gives up.

*Sometimes I get that and sometimes I am just all rigid about it.*

When there is no-one there is no need for difference, that's the difference.

All there is is what's happening and it doesn't
matter if that's an inhibition or a thought; it doesn't matter if it's dream-thinking, it is what's happening. The
frustration and anger of not getting this can be what's
happening. Resistance or non-resistance to this may
also be what's happening. Sitting on the seat, drinking
tea, walking, feeling warm, feeling cold, there is only
ever what is happening ... including deep sleep when
no-thing is what is happening. There is only being that
which is apparently happening.

We can't escape or attain or be aware of being; it
is simply what it is. It is totally open and it's totally
secret all the time there is an apparent seeking of it.
What is sought can never be known but has also never
been lost.

Meetings and residentials with Tony Parsons take place regularly in the UK and internationally.

For details, visit the website at:
http://www.theopensecret.com

Alternatively, you can write to Tony Parsons at:
PO Box 117, Shaftesbury, SP7 9WB, U.K.